AF411567

THE DEADLY DIRECTORY 2003

EDITED BY
KATE DERIE

DEADLY SERIOUS PRESS
TUCSON, ARIZONA

Although the editor and publisher have made every effort to ensure accuracy and completeness of information contained in this book, we assume no responsibility for errors, omissions, or inconsistencies herein. Listing of a business or organization does not imply recommendation or endorsement.

The Deadly Directory is published annually by Deadly Serious Press.
ISSN 1521-9690

Deadly Serious Press
6702 N Casas Adobes Dr
Tucson AZ 85704-6124
Website: www.deadlyserious.com
Email: info@deadlyserious.com

Contents

Introduction

WELCOME TO THE DEADLY DIRECTORY 2003!

Here is your guide to the mystery community—all the information you need to find everybody who is anybody in the world of mystery, crime, and suspense fiction and true crime writing.

The directory is divided into sections by category: booksellers, associations, events, etc. A summary of the categories and icons can be found following this introduction. Within each section, listings are alphabetical. New listings are denoted with a pistol ☞.

The appendix includes a chronological list of events, a glossary of acronyms, and the RIP section, which includes all listings dropped since the *Deadly Directory 2002*.

After the appendix, there is a detailed alphabetical index that includes: all listings; all contact names last name first *and* first name first (in case all you remember is "Willetta"); and all geographic locations—city, state/province, and country. We've also indexed certain authors, most newsletters, and a few useful cross-reference items. So, if you don't find what you're looking for in the categorized listings, check the index.

Descriptions. We've added icons so you can quickly skim for open stores, mail order, or online dealers. Mail order dealers generally accept phone, fax, or email orders, as well. Many mail order dealers also welcome visitors by appointment, so do telephone them if you will be in the neighborhood. Online ordering means secure shopping cart technology, not merely a catalog or an order form to email or fax.

Caveat: Lack of an icon does not necessarily mean that the service is not there—it may just mean we don't know about it. This is particularly true in the case of accessibility. Please phone first.

Bookseller membership in national and regional organizations has been noted in descriptions. Check the glossary in the appendix for translations.

International telephones. All phone numbers are listed with international prefixes. If you are outside of North America and telephoning within the same country, drop the international prefix (the first group of numbers, prefixed by a plus sign) and substitute "0." Consult your long-distance carrier for assistance in dialing an international call.

Corrections and additions. There were listing changes right up to the day this book went to the printer, and we're sure by the time you get it, there will be several more. Most of the descriptions are based on information provided by the listee. We strive for accuracy but make no guarantees. Listing in this directory does not imply recommendation or endorsement by the editor or publisher.

Please visit our website (www.DeadlySerious.com) often and pencil in any updates. If you have changes or additions to the listings, please let us know by email (info@deadly serious.com), or drop a note to Kate Derie, Deadly Serious Press, 6702 N Casas Adobes Dr, Tucson AZ 85704-6124.

Sherlockiana. If we included every existing Sherlockian organization, publication, or purveyor, this directory would be twice the size. So we have selected some of the longest established and most widely known, and hope that they will able to supply any further information desired. For the benefit of Sherlockian readers, we have used a special icon, §, for Sherlockian listings in every category, and indexed all mentions of Sherlock Holmes or Sherlockiana.

ABOUT ON-LINE BOOK SALES

You may notice that many of the websites for used and antiquarian booksellers start with www.abebooks.com. The Advanced Book Exchange (ABE) provides on-line book search and ordering services for over 5000 book dealers. You can look for a book title or author, and compare prices and descriptions from all member stores that have that book in stock. Or, you can locate a dealer and browse their catalog. When "also at ABE" is noted in a bookstore description, go to www.abe.com and click on the "Stores" tab to reach a search page.

You will see occasional references to "online at Amazon." However, it is does not appear to be possible to search for a specific bookstore; you must search for a book title or author instead. Alibris specializes in providing "hard-to-find" books to other booksellers, including Amazon and Books-A-Million, but you can also deal with them directly at www.alibris.com. TomFolio.com is a relatively small independent booksellers' cooperative, listing books for sale by several hundred member-owners.

Bookfinder.com remains an independent meta-search service. That means it searches all the book search services and provides you with choices from all of them (including ABE, Alibris, Amazon, TomFolio, and many more from around the world).

The Antiquarian Booksellers Association of America, cited in members' listings as ABAA, is a professional association of booksellers specializing in rare books. Their website, www.abaa.org, has links to members' online catalogs.

For new books, the American Booksellers Association (ABA) has BookSense.com, which provides secure on-line shopping from an independent bookstore in your neighborhood. Book Sense gift certificates can be used at any member store.

MAILING LABELS FROM DEADLY SERIOUS PRESS

Save yourself time and effort when sending a direct mailing about your new mystery book, event, product, or service. Just buy mailing labels from Deadly Serious Press and you will automatically get all the latest updates. They can be sorted any way you like—by zip, by category, by name, etc.

A set of labels including all current *Deadly Directory* listings (over 700) is $60, plus $4 postage to US and Canada ($9 to other countries). Subsets, such as publications only, are also available for 10¢ per label plus shipping (minimum charge $25). Labels (self-adhesive, laser-printed, 1″ x 2 5/8″) are sold for one-time use and may not be copied or duplicated. Electronic address files for unlimited use are available; please inquire about pricing to info@deadlyserious.com.

All addresses are deliverable to the best of our knowledge. We will refund 50¢ for each returned piece of mail if you send the item—or an email message—back to us so we can get the post office information. (That's one way we keep the listings current.)

To order labels or additional copies of the directory, visit www.DeadlySerious.com and order online using your credit card through the secure shopping technology of PayPal, or mail in your order with a check to Deadly Serious Press, 6702 N Casas Adobes Dr, Tucson AZ 85704-6124.

And don't forget to put us on your mailing list—we love to hear all the news.

Sections and Icons

BOOKSELLERS

Mystery specialists that carry new books (may also carry used).

+ Sellers of new books that specialize in mystery and other genres.

General independent booksellers with noteworthy mystery departments.

Booksellers that deal primarily in used, out-of-print, and collectible books.

Open store with regular hours.

Mail order dealer; telephone, fax, or email orders usually acceptable.

Secure online ordering available at website.

ASSOCIATIONS

Groups for writers and fans of mystery, crime, and detective fiction in general.

Groups that focus on a favorite character or author.

Internet newsgroups, website message forums, and electronic mailing lists.

EVENTS

Conventions, conferences, tours, and cruises.

Events that focus on a favorite character or author.

PERIODICALS & REVIEWERS

Magazines, newsletters, and journals that feature mystery fiction and/or related non-fiction: reviews, news, articles, interviews.

Author newsletters, published by one author or a group.

Newsletters and magazines that focus on a favorite character or author.

E-zines that provide mystery fiction and/or related articles, regularly updated.

Reviewers who specialize in reviewing mystery fiction, and the larger general book review publications.

INDEPENDENT PUBLISHERS

Independent publishers who specialize in mystery.

E-book publishers who feature mystery.

INFORMATION RESOURCES

Libraries, archives, and special collections of rare books, pulp fiction, manuscripts, and other material related to mystery fiction.

Websites that provide general mystery-related reference information.

ENTERTAINMENT & GIFTS

Mystery-theme events planners, dinner theaters, hotel weekends, party kits, etc.

Gifts for the mystery lover: jewelry, accessories, crafts, ephemera, and stuff.

Sources for audiobooks, original audio plays on cassette, and videotapes.

AWARDS

Awards for mystery fiction and related nonfiction, cross-referenced to the groups or events giving the award.

AND IN EVERY SECTION...

Sherlockian specialists.

New listings.

Booksellers

1MYSTERYSTREET.COM

171C Brush St	PHONE	1-707-463-1351
PO Box 8515	FAX	1-707-463-2072
Ukiah CA 95482-8515 USA	TOLLFREE	1-800-403-2665
	EMAIL	info@1Bookstreet.com
	WEBSITE	www.1MysteryStreet.com

🦅 ⌀ New books by mail. Online catalog with hundreds of new books listed by sub-genre, from British to amateur sleuths to mean streets. Bargains on remainders. Email newsletter. IMBA.

ABBEY'S BOOKSHOP

Peter Milne, Deputy Managing Direc-tor	PHONE	+61 2 9264 3111
	FAX	+61 2 9264 8993
131 York St	EMAIL	books@abbeys.com.au
Sydney NSW 2000 AUSTRALIA		

☼ 🏛 Area of shop devoted to "Crime Scene" with 6,000 titles including backlist. Monthly newsletter *Crime Chronicle,* free. ABA(AU).

☛ ABC BOOKS

Donus D Roberts	EMAIL	ddrabcbooks@hotmail.com
1281 2nd St NW		
Watertown SD 57201 USA		

🌙 🏛 ✉ Specializing in mystery, suspense, crime. Catalogues issued. Queries welcomed.

ACCESSORIES TO MURDER

Robin Elder	PHONE	1-310-792-0972
903 S Pacific Coast Hwy	FAX	1-310-792-5972
Redondo Beach CA 90277-4753 USA	TOLLFREE	1-877-740-MRDR
	EMAIL	info@accessoriestomurder.com
	WEBSITE	www.accessoriestomurder.com

🦅 🏛 Books, videos, and other assorted gift items. Gift baskets with books and other items. Author signings.

ACRES OF BOOKS

240 Long Beach Blvd	PHONE	1-562-437-6980
Long Beach CA 90802-3135 USA	EMAIL	jackie@acresofbooks.com

🌙 🏛 Astonishing quantity of used books (over 750,000) in a historic landmark building. Open daily. Bookstore cat: Penny.

ADVENTURES IN CRIME AND SPACE

Willie Siros, Owner	PHONE	1-512-383-1376
shipping:	EMAIL	acs@crimeandspace.com
1504 Norris Dr	WEBSITE	www.CrimeAndSpace.com
Austin TX 78704 USA		
mailing:		
PO Box 684608		
Austin TX 78768-4608 USA		

🦉+ ⌀ Online and by appointment only. Specializing in mystery, science fiction, & horror books. New, used, and rare. Newsletter by email. ABA, IMBA.

AL JAMIESON - FIRST EDITIONS

814 S Nelson Way	PHONE	1-303-980-1704
Lakewood CO 80226-3860 USA	EMAIL	alwjamieson@attbi.com

☽ ✉ ⌀ Mystery, literature. Used, new, collectible, many signed. Mail order; online at ABE. Also at Denver Book Mall 🏛 ♿, 32 Broadway, 303-733-3808. RMABA.

ALIBI BOOKS

Sheri Kraft	PHONE	1-847-657-7832
995 Waukegan Rd #B	FAX	1-847-657-7848
Glenview IL 60025-4314 USA	EMAIL	info@alibibooks.com
	WEBSITE	www.alibibooks.com

☀ 🏛 New books. Large mystery & suspense selection. Newsletter, frequent buyer discount. ABA, IMBA, Book Sense.

ALLWEST BOOKS

Ralph & Yvonne Richardson	PHONE	1-818-884-4800
23716 Strathern St	EMAIL	allwest@earthlink.net
West Hills CA 91304-5712 USA		

☽ 🏛 First editions, collectible, rare. Modern mystery & detective fiction. Catalog available.

ALMARK & CO—BOOKSELLERS

Al Navis & Mark Novak	PHONE	1-905-764-2665
PO Box 7	FAX	1-905-764-5571
Thornhill ON L3T 3N1 CANADA	EMAIL	almark-co@rogers.com
	WEBSITE	www.almarkco.com

☽ ✉ Will print stock lists on demand by author & subgenre. "More up to date." All genres in addition to mystery. Open by appointment, please telephone. ABAC, ILAB, CBA, CWC, MWA, CWA, IACW.

ALOTTABOOKS.COM

Bill Walton	PHONE	1-856-456-7665
112 Nicholson Rd	FAX	1-856-456-7675
Gloucester City NJ 08030-1225 USA	EMAIL	mailto@alottabooks.com
	WEBSITE	www.alottabooks.com

☽ ⌀ Internet-only bookseller with over 160,000 books. Mysteries a specialty. ABAA.

ALPHABET BOOKSHOP

Richard D Shuh & Linda Wooley
145 Main St W
Port Colborne ON L3K 3V3 CANADA

PHONE/FAX 1-905-834-5323
EMAIL info@alphabet-bookshop.com
WEBSITE www.alphabet-bookshop.com

⟨ ✉ ∅ Modern first editions, rare books, mystery & detective fiction. Mail/email/phone order or by appointment. Online sales through ABE. Appraisal services. ABAC, ILAB.

AM RAND

Barbara Schneider
Röschibachstrasse 73
8037 Zürich SWITZERLAND

PHONE +41 1 271 2151

🦅 🏛 At the Edge. Primarily new mysteries.

THE AMERICAN BOOK CENTER

main store:
Kalverstraat 185
1012 XC Amsterdam NETHERLANDS
The Hague:
Lange Poten 23
2511 CM Den Haag NETHERLANDS
Belgium:
Diestsestraat 115
3000 Leuven BELGIUM

PHONE +31 20 625 5537
FAX +31 20 624 8042
EMAIL info@abc.nl
WEBSITE www.abc.nl

☼ 🏛 The largest source of English language books in Europe. Large mystery department.

ANDERSON'S BOOKSHOP

Doris Blechman
123 W Jefferson
Naperville IL 60567 USA

PHONE 1-630-355-2665
FAX 1-630-820-0057
TOLLFREE 1-800-728-0708
EMAIL andersons@andersonsbooks.com
WEBSITE www.andersonsbookshop.com

☼ 🏛 Longtime mystery bookseller Doris Blechman has expanded the mystery section at this local independent. Author signings.

ANDREA'S BOOKSTORE

Andrea Gillean
308 S State Road 19
Palatka FL 32177-3939 USA

PHONE 1-904-325-2141
FAX 1-904-325-8352
EMAIL andrea@gbso.net
WEBSITE www.andreasbookstore.com

☼ 🏛 General bookstore located east of Gainesville. Hosts author signings with big media promotion.

ANDY'S BOOKS

Andy Langwiser	PHONE	1-714-527-6935
PO Box 2686	FAX	1-714-527-4263
Cypress CA 90630-1386 USA	EMAIL	andysbks@earthlink.net
	WEBSITE	www.abebooks.com/home/andysbks/

First editions, from new to rare, with a strong mystery department. Many signed. Catalog available. Mail order, online, or by appointment only. Also at ABE.

ANN'S BOOKS & MOSTLY MYSTERIES

Ann & David Skene-Melvin
30 Elm Ave #210
Toronto ON M4W 1N5 CANADA

Mail order only. Used, collectible & rare Canadian crime fiction.

ANTIKVARIAATTI SYVÄ UNI

Matti & Pertti Seppälä	PHONE/FAX	+358 9 693 3939
Fredrikinkatu 55	EMAIL	antikvariaatti.syva.uni@kolumbus.fi
00100 Helsinki FINLAND	WEBSITE	www.kolumbus.fi/ antikvariaatti.syva.uni/

Antiquarian bookshop has a fair selection of classic and modern detective fiction in Finnish translation and in English. Online catalog & email ordering. Website in English & Finnish. ILAB.

AS CRIME GOES BY, A MYSTERY BOOKSTORE

Kathryn Rubio, Owner	PHONE	1-208-853-4225
PO Box 140758	EMAIL	krubio@rmci.net
Boise ID 83714-0758 USA		

Est. 1998. Specializing in both new and used mysteries, true crime, paperbacks, collectible literature.

AT VICKI'S BOOKS

Vicki E Hall	PHONE	1-501-985-0670
store:	EMAIL	vickibooks@aristotle.net
100 Municipal Dr	WEBSITE	www.abebooks.com/home/ vickibooks/
Jacksonville AR 72076 USA		
mail-order:		
1509 Elaine Dr		
Jacksonville AR 72076-3670 USA		

Specializing in mystery, suspense, and thrillers. Small open store sells mainly paperbacks. Online sales include modern first editions and collectible hardcovers. Many signed copies. New, gently used, ARCs, used & collectible books. ABA, SEBA, MSIBA.

AUGUSTINE FUNNELL BOOKS

PO Box 20171
Kings Place Postal Outlet
Fredericton NB E3B 7A2 CANADA

PHONE 1-506-472-2053
EMAIL gobruins@nbnet.nb.ca
WEBSITE www.gusbooks.com

Online and mail-order; open by appointment only. General stock with good selection of mystery hardcovers and vintage paperbacks.

AUNT AGATHA'S

Jamie & Robin Agnew
213 S 4th Ave
Ann Arbor MI 48104-2134 USA

PHONE 1-734-769-1114
EMAIL auntagathas@excite.com

New and used mystery, detective, & true crime. Gifts, games, etc. Mystery reading club. IMBA.

AVENUE VICTOR HUGO BOOKSHOP

Vincent McCaffery
353 Newbury St
Boston MA 02115-2710 USA

PHONE 1-617-266-7746
FAX 1-617-266-1137
EMAIL books@avenuevictorhugobooks.com
WEBSITE www.avenuevictorhugobooks.com

General stock, mostly used, with strong collection of mysteries. New location a few doors from old location. Monthly email newsletter. Online sales with ABE and BookSense. ABA. Bookstore cat: Blue Bart.

☛ BABCOCK BOOKS

Bert Babcock
9 E Derry Rd
PO Box 1140
Derry NH 03038 USA

PHONE 1-603-432-9142
FAX 1-603-425-6580
EMAIL contact@babcockbooks.com
WEBSITE www.babcockbooks.com

Mail order or by appointment. Modern first editions in mainstream and genre fiction. Online catalog shows a good selection of signed mysteries. Print catalogs available, want lists welcome. Will appraise and purchase books and collections. ABAA, ILAB.

BASKERVILLE BÜCHER

Michael Ross
Postfach 42 06 70
50900 Köln GERMANY

PHONE/FAX +49 221 475 8063
WEBSITE www.baskerville.de

Specializing in Sherlock Holmes. New & used books by mail, catalog available, want-lists welcome. Also a publisher of Sherlockiana and mystery studies. Website in German.

BEARLY READ BOOKS

David & Jane Van Buskirk	PHONE	1-978-443-4034
320 Boston Post Rd	FAX	1-978-440-9527
Sudbury MA 01776-3007 USA	EMAIL	bearly@rcn.com

⟨ ∅ 50,000 used, out-of-print, collectible, modern first editions. Many mysteries, also children's, military, local history, nautical, aviation. Two cats.

BENGTA WOO BOOKS

1 Sorgi Ct	PHONE	1-516-692-4426
Plainview NY 11803-1822 USA	EMAIL	bengtabks@aol.com

⟨ ✉ Mail order and by appointment, specializing in mystery. Used, firsts, rare. Hardcover & paper, 15,000 titles. Want lists welcome.

☛ BETWEEN THE COVERS RARE BOOKS

Tom Congalton	PHONE	1-856-665-2284
35 W Maple Ave	FAX	1-856-665-3639
Merchantville NJ 08109 USA	EMAIL	mail@betweenthecovers.com
	WEBSITE	www.betweenthecovers.com

⟨ ⌂ ✉ ∅ Open store but telephone to check schedule. Large (30,000) selection of books, mostly modern firsts, with specialties including genre fiction, and African-American. Online catalog has good-sized photographs of most books available at your option. 6-8 print catalogs per year, available by subscription. ABAA, ILAB.

BIG SLEEP BOOKS

Helen Simpson	PHONE	1-314-361-6100
239 N Euclid Ave	EMAIL	bigsleep.books@slacc.com
Saint Louis MO 63108-1527 USA	WEBSITE	www.bigsleepbooks.com

🦅 ⌂ Mystery, espionage, true crime, suspense. New & used, first editions. Newsletter, signings. Store guard dog: Rudi the Rudemeister (mini-dachsund).

BIRD & BECKETT BOOKS & RECORDS

Eric Whittington	PHONE	1-415-586-3733
2788 Diamond St	FAX	1-415-586-3739
San Francisco CA 94131-3057 USA	EMAIL	birdbeckett@earthlink.net

☼ ⌂ New independent store with new, used, & rare books. Hosts mystery author signings. Closed Mondays. NCIBA.

BLACK AND WHITE BOOKS

Rushton H Potts	PHONE	1-508-862-0500
100 W Main St # 5	EMAIL	bwbooks@attbi.com
Hyannis MA 02601-3777 USA	WEBSITE	www.abebooks.com/home/ bwbooks2/

⟨ ✉ ∅ Mail or email order only. Used, firsts & rare. Mystery, detective, SF, fantasy. Reference. Facsimile dustjackets available. Frequent catalogs. Est. 1986.

BLACK BIRD MYSTERIES

Kathleen Riley
PO Box 444
Keedysville MD 21756-0444 USA

PHONE 1-301-432-8781
FAX 1-301-432-8782
TOLLFREE 1-800-449-7709
EMAIL info@blackbird-mysteries.com
WEBSITE www.blackbird-mysteries.com

Specializing in Golden Age mysteries including vintage paperbacks, firsts & collectible hardcovers; plus new and used titles. Free monthly e-newsletter. Secure online ordering, phone, mail or email. Visits by appointment only. IMBA.

BLACK DOG MYSTERY FIRSTS

Ronald Kester
1133 99th St
Everett WA 98205-1910 USA

PHONE 1-425-377-9889
FAX 1-425-377-9120
EMAIL kester15@yahoo.com
WEBSITE www.abebooks.com/home/
kester15/

Internet sales only. First edition mysteries, suspense, thriller & espionage. Out-of-print searches gladly.

BLACK HILL BOOKS

Jean & Guy N Smith, Proprietors
The Wain House
Black Hill, Clunton
Craven Arms, Shropshire SY7 0JD
ENGLAND

PHONE/FAX +44 1588 640551
EMAIL blackhillbooks@hotmail.com
WEBSITE www.abebooks.com/home/
blackhillbooks

Mail order only. Large stock of used & rare hardback & softcover crime, mystery, & horror. Monthly catalogues. Open for viewing by appointment.

THE BLACK ORCHID BOOKSHOP

Bonnie Claeson & Joe Guglielmelli
303 E 81st St
New York NY 10028-4000 USA

PHONE 1-212-734-5980
FAX 1-212-288-5918
EMAIL BOrchid@aol.com
WEBSITE www.ageneralstore.com

Signed first editions, bargain h/c, obscure p/b. UK imports. In an old brownstone. Many author events.

BLACKWOOD & BROUWER BOOKSELLERS

Jean Brower
7 Hudson St
PO Box 767
Kinderhook NY 12106-0767 USA

PHONE 1-518-758-1232
EMAIL bbbltd@kinderhookconnection.com
WEBSITE www.kinderhookconnection.com/
bbbltd/

General shop with a good selection of mysteries, children's, & regional. Gifts, special orders. SinC, ABA, NEBA.

BLUE PARROT BOOKS

Linda & Richard Taylor	PHONE	1-316-265-6900
816 W 13th St N	TOLLFREE	1-866-446-6324
Wichita KS 67203-3406 USA	EMAIL	bluparotbk@aol.com
	WEBSITE	www.abebooks.com/home/ blueparrot

⟨ 🏛 ⌀ Open store in historic Riverside district. Mostly used books, with a small selection of new books. About one-third of stock is mystery/thrillers. Online sales through ABE.

BLUE SKY BOOKS

Bill Mooney, Owner	PHONE	1-415-921-7972
1821 Polk St #7	EMAIL	billmooney@worldnet.att.net
San Francisco CA 94109-3026 USA	WEBSITE	www.abebooks.com/home/blue_sky/

⟨ ✉ ⌀ Mail order. Crime fiction 1890–1990. Catalog available. Used, firsts, collectible, rare. ABAA.

BMD BOOKS

Marilyn West, Owner	PHONE	1-936-294-9034
PO Box 8007	EMAIL	bmdbooks@bmdbooks.com
Huntsville TX 77340-0001 USA	WEBSITE	www.bmdbooks.com

⟨ ✉ ⌀ Specializing in first edition mysteries and SF/fantasy from Victorian era to present. Online/mail order/by appointment only.

THE BOOK BARON

Bob Weinstein, Owner	PHONE	1-714-527-7022
1236 S Magnolia Ave	FAX	1-714-527-5634
Anaheim CA 92804-5116 USA	EMAIL	bookbaron1@bookbaron.com
	WEBSITE	www.bookbaron.com

☼ 🏛 ♿ ✉ ⌀ General bookstore with large mystery collection—collectible, used & rare. Also Magazine Baron with large stock of vintage periodicals. Mail order & online sales, want lists, books searches. Occasional catalogs. Branches in Long Beach and Fullerton.

BOOK CARNIVAL: MYSTERY & DARK FANTASY

Ed & Pat Thomas, Owners	PHONE	1-714-538-3210
348 S Tustin Ave	FAX	1-714-538-3273
Orange CA 92866-2502 USA	EMAIL	bookcarnival@earthlink.net
	WEBSITE	home.earthlink.net/~bookcarnival/

🖋+ 🏛 ♿ Large collection of new & used, firsts & rare. Many signings. Store mascot: Mr. Bones.

BOOK HOUSE OF STUYVESANT PLAZA

Julia Payne & Dan Schreffler
1475 Western Ave
Albany NY 12203-3586 USA

PHONE 1-518-489-4761
FAX 1-518-489-4318
EMAIL bookhouse@bhny.com
WEBSITE www.bhny.com

☼ 🏛 Hosts mystery reading group, author signings. Email newsletter. ABA, NEBA.

THE BOOK ORPHANAGE

Jeff Kreider
210 N Iris Ave
Rialto CA 92376-5727 USA

PHONE 1-909-874-6214
FAX 1-909-874-2143
EMAIL jeff@book-orphanage.com
WEBSITE www.book-orphanage.com

🦅 ✉ On-line catalog of first editions, signed and unsigned, specializing in mystery. New, used, reading copies. Synopsis/Reviewlettes in the "Slow Reader's Quarterly Reports" posted on the web site.

BOOK PASSAGE

Elaine & Bill Petrocelli, Owners
51 Tamal Vista Blvd
Corte Madera CA 94925-1145 USA

PHONE 1-415-927-0960
FAX 1-415-924-3838
TOLLFREE 1-800-999-7909
EMAIL store@bookpassage.com
WEBSITE www.bookpassage.com

☼ 🏛 ∅ New, used, & rentals with large mystery section. Active author event schedule, writing classes & conferences, book clubs, café. Pays author royalties on used books. Biweekly email newsletter, active website. Annual **Book Passage Mystery Writers' Conference**. ABA, NCIBA.

THE BOOK SHOPPE

Kelly Chandler, Manager
1822 W Berry St
Fort Worth TX 76110-3403 USA

PHONE 1-817-926-8208
EMAIL bookshop@thebookshoppe.com
WEBSITE www.thebookshoppe.com

🦅 🏛 ♿ Used & rare books since 1987. General selections with many mysteries, and mystery fans on staff. Website updated monthly, occasional newsletters & catalogs by mail. Want lists welcomed. Cats: Simon & Schuster. NTBA.

BOOK SLEUTH MYSTERY BOOKSTORE

Helen Randal, Owner
2501 W Colorado Ave Ste 105
Colorado Springs CO 80904-3000
  USA

PHONE 1-719-632-2727
EMAIL mysterybooks@OldColoradoCity.com

🦅 🏛 ♿ Only mystery bookstore in southern Colorado. New and used h/c and p/b. Signings, newsletter *The Casebook*. ABA, IMBA. Cats: Sherlock and Moriarty.

BOOK TRADER

Jo Ann Saxton, Owner	PHONE	1-405-787-7171
4530 NW 50th St		
Oklahoma City OK 73122-5331		
USA		

♪ 🏛 Used books, mostly reader's copies, with large mystery section. Some firsts & new paperbacks.

BOOK TREE

Barry & Terry Phillips	PHONE	1-972-437-4337
702 University Village Ctr	EMAIL	BookTree@aol.com
Richardson TX 75081-3867 USA	WEBSITE	www.booktree.net

☀ 🏛 ⊘ Primarily used, some new, paperback books in popular and genre fiction. Collectible out-of-print hardcover mysteries. Online catalog and sales.

BOOK'EM (NEWPORT RI)

Andy & Mary Rosenzweig	PHONE	1-401-849-5589
433 Thames St	EMAIL	BookEmRI@aol.com
Newport RI 02840 USA		

☀ 🏛 Listed for reference only. Small general-interest bookstore. No events. NEBA.

BOOK'EM MYSTERIES (SOUTH PASADENA CA)

Barry Martin & Mary Riley	PHONE	1-626-799-9600
1118 Mission St	FAX	1-626-799-9605
South Pasadena CA 91030-3212 USA	TOLLFREE	1-800-4BOOKEM
	EMAIL	mystery@bookem.com
	WEBSITE	www.bookem.com

🐒 🏛 New mysteries and crime fiction, selected better fiction & Book Sense 76, first edition collectibles, used paperbacks. Many author events. Newsletter. ABA.

BOOKDALES

David Dale	PHONE	1-612-861-3303
PO Box 23900	EMAIL	bkdales@aol.com
Richfield MN 55423-0900 USA	WEBSITE	www.abebooks.com/home/ bookdales/

♪ ✉ ⊘ General used, rare, firsts & out of print. Hard & soft. Mystery emphasis. Shop open by appointment.

BOOKED FOR MURDER, LTD

Paul Houseman	PHONE	1-608-238-2701
2701 University Ave	FAX	1-608-238-1326
Madison WI 53705-3700 USA	TOLLFREE	1-800-200-5996
	EMAIL	booked4murder@mailbag.com
	WEBSITE	www.bookedformurder.com

🐒 🏛 New, used, and collectible books. Mystery, suspense, espionage, children's mysteries, games, puzzles, gift baskets, etc. IMBA, ABA.

BOOKFEVER.COM

Christine Volk & Shep Iiams	PHONE	1-209-274-6960
PO Box 696	EFAX	1-617-812-5371
Ione CA 95640-0696 USA	TOLLFREE	1-877-BOOKFEVER
	EMAIL	heyyou@bookfever.com
	WEBSITE	www.bookfever.com

☾ ✉ Mystery & detective, modern firsts, SF/fantasy. Rare, used, out-of-print. Catalogs available. Primarily mail order, open by appointment. Selection of stock at The Book Collector, 1008 24th St, Sacramento, CA, or at Books Upstairs, 5 Main St, Jackson, CA.

BOOKS ARE EVERYTHING!

Graham Holroyd	EMAIL	gholroyd@rochester.rr.com
31 Lancer Pl	WEBSITE	www.booksareeverything.com
Webster NY 14580 USA		

☾ ✉ ∅ Fast service by mail order and Internet only. Over 200,000 paperbacks, primarily from 1938 to 1970, and modern collectibles. All genres. New owner.

BOOKS & COMPANY (DAYTON OH)

Lou LaLa	PHONE	1-937-298-6540
350 E Stroop Rd	FAX	1-937-297-6483
Dayton OH 45429-2885 USA	TOLLFREE	1-800-843-2028

☼ 🏛 ∅ Largest in the region—over 35,000 sq. ft. Signings. Monthly mystery reading group. Author events. Online shopping through Books-a-Million.

BOOKS & COMPANY (OCONOMOWOC WI)

Beth Fedyn	PHONE	1-262-567-0106
1039 Summit Ave	EMAIL	info@booksco.com
Oconomowoc WI 53066-4457 USA	WEBSITE	www.booksco.com

☼ 🏛 Knowledgeable mystery fan runs a strong mystery department in this independent bookstore. Reading groups, mystery and general newsletters. ABA, Book Sense.

BOOKS 'N' STUFF

Susan I Warren	PHONE	1-910-457-9017
4961 Live Oak Shopping Ctr #11	FAX	1-910-457-9612
Southport NC 28461-8708 USA	EMAIL	booksnstuff@juno.com

☼ 🏛 New & used bookstore, combined with typing and writing service.

BOOKS OF MOBILE

Cristy & Gregory Yarborough	PHONE	1-251-344-6205
PO Box 851173	EMAIL	BooksOfMobile@bkseller.com
Mobile AL 36685 USA	WEBSITE	www.bkseller.com

☾ ✉ Used, collectible, out of print. Hardcover & paperback. Fiction, especially mysteries & historical fiction. Also espionage and spy thrillers, action adventure novels, religious books, self-help books, & rare tomes.

BOOKS

Mary Anne Ramirez, Owner	PHONE	1-602-678-4576
9201 N 7th Ave	EMAIL	Bkfinder@aol.com
Phoenix AZ 85021-3518 USA	WEBSITE	www.BookMar.com

☾ ⌂ Phoenix's largest used bookstore. Over 150,000 titles in stock. Hardcover, paperbacks. Store mascot: Jane, a beautiful green parrotlet.

BOOKS WEST

Judith C Hurley	PHONE	1-916-331-4746
PO Box 417760	FAX	1-916-332-5457
Sacramento CA 95841-7760 USA	EMAIL	bookswst@calweb.com
	WEBSITE	www.abebooks.com/home/ bookmite/

☾ ✉ ⌀ Reader's copies of used paperback, vintage paperback, and hardcover mysteries. Online sales through ABE.

THE BOOKSHELF

Denise Nelson	PHONE	1-512-868-2193
101 Luther Dr #109	WEBSITE	www.abebooks.com/home/ bkshelfs/
Georgetown TX 78628-8775 USA		
	EMAIL	the.bookshelf@verizon.net
	EMAIL	bookshelf@cox-internet.com

☾ ⌂ ⌀ Shop specializing in used, first edition, and collectible mysteries along with general selection.

BOUND TO BE READ

Jackie Melton, Mystery Buyer	PHONE	1-505-828-3500
Far North Shopping Ctr	FAX	1-505-828-3502
6300 San Mateo Blvd NE	TOLLFREE	1-800-688-4041
Albuquerque NM 87109-3530 USA	EMAIL	Bound2bRea@aol.com

☀ ⌂ Independent bookstore with coffee & leisure seating. Good mysteries. ABA.

BRAIN SNACKS

Sue Petersen, Owner	PHONE	1-630-241-1040
5221 Main St	FAX	1-630-241-1043
Downers Grove IL 60515-4614 USA	EMAIL	brnsncks@aol.com
	WEBSITE	www.brnsncks.com

☀ ⌂ In Green Knolls Shopping Center. Mystery, romance, SF/fantasy. Rubber stamps, role playing games. Special orders welcome, frequent-buyer discount.

B. BROWN AND ASSOCIATES

Bob Brown	PHONE	1-206-634-1481
3534 Stone Way N	FAX	1-206-634-1484
Seattle WA 98103-8924 USA	EMAIL	bobbrown@wolfenet.com
	WEBSITE	www.bbrownandassoc.com

☾ ⌂ Fine used and rare books. Mystery, horror, supernatural, SF, fantasy, and more. 90% hardcover, many signed. Want lists welcome; will quote.

☞ BROWN'S BOOKS HOUSE OF MYSTERY

3740 Hastings Street	PHONE	1-604-204-9311
Burnaby BC V5C 2H5 CANADA	EMAIL	brownsbooks@hotmail.com

Large collection of new and used mysteries. Author signings.

BUCKINGHAM BOOKS

Lew & Nancy Buckingham, Owners	PHONE	1-717-597-5657
8058 Stone Bridge Rd	FAX	1-717-597-1003
Greencastle PA 17225-9786 USA	EMAIL	buckingham@innernet.net
	WEBSITE	www.buckinghambooks.com

Mail order, online, and by appointment only. New, used, collectible & rare mystery, detective, espionage & adventure fiction. Bibliomysteries, historical mysteries, and UK editions a specialty. Frequent catalogs. ABAA, IOBA.

BUFFALO MEDICINE BOOKS

Ernie Bulow	PHONE	1-505-722-2904
PO Box 1762	FAX	1-505-722-3465
Gallup NM 87305-1762 USA	EMAIL	ernie@buffalomedicine.com
	WEBSITE	www.buffalomedicine.com

General stock of mystery fiction, with specialty in Native American and Southwestern interest books. Signed first editions. Online sales.

CANDLESTICK BOOKS

Charles Peterson	PHONE	1-413-528-4281
PO Box 27	EMAIL	peterson@candlestickbooks.com
South Egremont MA 01258-0027	WEBSITE	www.abebooks.com/home/
USA		candlestick/

Specializing in mystery and suspense, exploration, literature, natural history, modern firsts. Visitors welcome by appointment.

CANFORD BOOK CORRAL

Mike Cancellari	PHONE	1-607-844-9784
Drawer 216	EMAIL	mcancell@twcny.rr.com
Freeville NY 13068-0216 USA	WEBSITE	www.abebooks.com/home/canford/

Catalog of mystery & detective fiction. Specializes in first editions from 1900 to 1970s. Also SF, fantasy, & western fiction catalogs. Mail, email, or online ordering.

CAPITAL CRIMES MYSTERY BOOKSTORE

Joe Morales, Owner	PHONE	1-916-441-4798
PO Box 218	EMAIL	books@capitalcrimes.com
Sacramento CA 95617-0218 USA		

New and used mysteries by mail order (store closed). First editions & collectibles, vintage paperbacks. IMBA.

CARDINAL BOOKS

Larry & Linda Johnson	PHONE	1-360-576-9070
4010 NE 136th St	FAX	1-360-576-0475
Vancouver WA 98686-2614 USA	EMAIL	cardinalbo@aol.com

(✉ Firsts, collectible & rare. Mystery & crime fiction specialist. Mail order only, catalog available.

CEMETERY PLOTS

JoAnne Bowers	EMAIL	mamacat@earthlink.net
2913 Division St	WEBSITE	home.earthlink.net/~mamacat/
Blossvale NY 13308-2609 USA		

(✉ Email ordering only, from online catalog. Collectible modern mysteries, many signed, and a large assortment of mystery reading copies.

CENTRAL BOOKING

Lola Troy Fiur	PHONE/FAX	1-212-861-1911
360 E 65th St #17a	EMAIL	ltfoto@bellatlantic.net
New York NY 10021-6724 USA		

(✉ Mail order only. Specializing in mystery & related genre. New, used, firsts, & out-of-print. Ephemera. Want lists welcome.

CENTURIES & SLEUTHS BOOKSTORE

August Paul Aleksy Jr	PHONE	1-708-771-7243
7419 W Madison St	FAX	1-708-771-7412
Forest Park IL 60130-1502 USA	EMAIL	augitraj@aol.com
	WEBSITE	www.centuriesandsleuths.com

+ ⌂ ✉ Mystery, history & biography, children's. Tapes, gifts, signings. Active discussion groups who stage plays & dramatic readings. Shop also does mail order, special orders, free gift wrap. Celebrating over 10 years as an independent bookseller. ABA, Book Sense.

CHC BOOKS, UK

Chris Calvert	PHONE/FAX	+44 1638 713297
75 Charles Melrose Close	EMAIL	chcbooks@enterprise.net
Mildenhall, Suffolk IP28 7BA	WEBSITE	www.ukfirsteditions.com
ENGLAND		

✉ Mail order or by appt. Mystery, crime, detective, thriller, adventure and especially authors' first novels. Large stock, mainly new UK & US hypermodern firsts. Quarterly catalogs.

CHRIS ECKHOFF BOOKS

98 Pierrepont St
Brooklyn NY 11201-2718 USA

(✉ Mail order only, vintage paperbacks, all genres. Crime & espionage fiction and nonfiction.

CHRISTINE KOVACH, BOOKSELLER

10814 Harvest Sun Dr	PHONE	1-281-807-1660
Houston TX 77064-4489 USA	EMAIL	books@kovachbooks.com
	WEBSITE	www.kovachbooks.com

Specializes in mystery, Sherlockiana, SF & horror. Used, firsts, & rare. Mail order, online catalog & sales. Home of Cujo the Wonder Cat.

CLASSIC BOOK SHOP

David Oyerly, Manager	PHONE	1-248-549-0220
32336 Woodward Ave	TOLLFREE	1-866-215-0829
Royal Oak MI 48073-0945 USA	EMAIL	classicbooks@earthlink.net

General bookstore with good selection of used, rare, and first editions. Online sales at ABE.

CLAUDE HELD, BOOKSELLER

PO Box 515
Buffalo NY 14225-0515 USA

Firsts, used, collectible, and rare books. Mystery, SF, fantasy, pulp magazines, EQMMs. Catalog available.

A CLEAN WELL-LIGHTED PLACE FOR BOOKS

Leona Weiss	PHONE	1-415-441-6670
601 Van Ness Ave	FAX	1-415-567-6885
San Francisco CA 94102-3272 USA	EMAIL	books@bookstore.com
	WEBSITE	www.bookstore.com

Good selection of new mystery fiction & reference. Chosen best San Francisco bookstore. Author signings. ABA, NCIBA.

CLOAK & DAGGER BOOKS (MONSEY NY)

79 Regina Rd	PHONE	1-914-371-6739
Monsey NY 10952-4527 USA	FAX	1-914-371-4381
	EMAIL	siralewker@aol.com

Mail order only. Golden Era hardcover mysteries and vintage paperback mysteries plus occasional surprises.

CLOAK & DAGGER BOOKS (SHIPPENSBURG PA)

Robert M Wynne, Proprietor	PHONE	1-717-532-8213
227 Lurgan Ave		
Shippensburg PA 17257-1625 USA		

'30s, '40s, & '50s hardcover, '50s & '60s paperbacks. Catalogs available.

CLOAK AND DAGGER BOOKS (BEDFORD NH)

Dan Halpin	PHONE	1-603-668-1629
9 Eastman Ave	FAX	1-603-626-0626
Bedford NH 03110-6701 USA	EMAIL	cloakandspies@juno.com
	WEBSITE	www.cloakanddagger.com/dagger/

◖ ✉ Non-fiction only. World's largest dealer in intelligence literature. New, out-of-print, and hard-to-find non-fiction books on espionage, military intelligence, codes & ciphers, terrorism, political assassinations, etc. Mail or fax order; open by appointment or chance.

THE CLOAK AND DAGGER (PRINCETON NJ)

Aline Lenaz, Owner	PHONE	1-609-688-9840
349 Nassau St	FAX	1-609-688-9844
Princeton NJ 08540-4614 USA	EMAIL	info@thecloakanddagger.com
	WEBSITE	www.thecloakanddagger.com

🦅 🏬 Paperbacks & trade paper; new & used. Children's mysteries, large print. Mystery puzzles, how-to-host-a-murder games, audio, video, DVDs, accessories & gifts. Author signings. Special orders welcome. IMBA, ABA.

CLUES UNLIMITED

Chris & Marcelino Acevedo	PHONE	1-520-326-8533
123 S Eastbourne Dr #16	FAX	1-520-326-9001
Tucson AZ 85716-5317 USA	EMAIL	info@cluesunlimited.com
	WEBSITE	www.cluesunlimited.com

🦅 🏬 ♿ New and collectible. Arrangement with bookstore in England makes this a good source of British fiction. ABA, MPBA, IMBA. Store mascot is Sophie the pot-bellied pig.

CODY'S BOOKS

Andy Ross, Owner	PHONE	1-510-845-7852
2454 Telegraph Ave	FAX	1-510-841-6185
Berkeley CA 94704-2320 USA	TOLLFREE	1-800-995-1180
	EMAIL	info@codysbooks.com
	WEBSITE	www.codysbooks.com

☼ 🏬 Famously independent, activist bookstore. One of America's largest. New books, large mystery section. Many UK editions. Reading group, author signings. California toll-free 800-479-7744. ABA, NCIBA.

COFFEE, TEA & MYSTERY

Joan Wunsch, Owner	PHONE	1-714-898-2583
11931 Valley View St	FAX	1-714-892-4437
Garden Grove CA 92845-1238 USA	EMAIL	ctmbooks@worldnet.att.net
	WEBSITE	www.ctmbooks.com

🦅 🏬 ♿ New books, gifts, puzzles, Sherlockian, etc. Antiques & coffee bar. Many author signings & special events. Bimonthly newsletter. ABA.

THE COLOPHON BOOK SHOP

Robert & Christine Liska	PHONE	1-603-772-8443
mailing:	FAX	1-603-772-3384
PO Box 1052	EMAIL	colophon@nh.ultranet.com
Exeter NH 03833-1052 USA	WEBSITE	www.colophonbooks.com

store:
72 Portsmouth Ave
Stratham Plaza
Stratham NH 03885-2566 USA

Est. 1971. Mystery & detective fiction and literary first editions, and "books about books." ABAA, ILAB, NHABA.

COOK INLET BOOK COMPANY

Ron & Lynn Dixon, Owners	PHONE	1-907-258-4544
415 W 5th Ave	FAX	1-907-258-4491
Anchorage AK 99501-2309 USA	TOLLFREE	1-800-240-4148
	EMAIL	info@cookinlet.com
	WEBSITE	www.cookinlet.com

The 49th state's largest independent bookseller features Alaskan mystery writers as well as other Alaskana. Shop also offers mail order and online sales.

THE CORNER SHOP

Margaret Cheeseman, Owner	PHONE/FAX	1-219-726-4090

116 E Water St
Portland IN 47371-2111 USA

Mostly used, some new books, general with mystery emphasis. First editions & reader's copies. Search and alert services. Accessible but with one small incline.

THE CORNSTALK BOOKSHOP

Paul Feain	PHONE	+61 2 9660 4889
112 Glebe Point Road	FAX	+61 2 9552 2670
PO Box 336 Glebe	EMAIL	books@cornstalk.com.au
Sydney NSW 2037 AUSTRALIA	WEBSITE	www.cornstalk.com.au

Open store, closed weekends. Good source for collectible Australian and British crime fiction. Catalog available.

CREATURES 'N CROOKS BOOKSHOPPE

Lelia Taylor	PHONE	1-804-330-4111
9762 Midlothian Turnpike	FAX	1-804-330-4005
Richmond VA 23235 USA	TOLLFREE	1-888-533-5303
	EMAIL	info@cncbooks.com
	WEBSITE	www.cncbooks.com

Mystery, true crime, science fiction, fantasy and horror for adults and children. Preferred reader's discount club, reading groups, events. Newsletter by mail or on website. Special orders. ABA, IMBA, MWA, SinC. Cat named Hamilton (the boss).

CRIME EXPRESS

Dr Stephan Schölzel
Am Wiembusch 18
58135 Hagen GERMANY
  ☽ ✉ Mail order books.

PHONE/FAX +49 2331 40 35 28

CRIME IN STORE

Geoffrey Bailey & Thalia Proctor
32 Store Street
(Off Tottenham Court Road)
London WC1E 7BS ENGLAND

PHONE +44 207 436 7736
FAX +44 207 436 7636
EMAIL CrimeBks@aol.com
WEBSITE www.crimeinstore.co.uk

  Mystery specialists, also true crime, Sherlockiana, sea and adventure. New, used, and collectible. Quarterly catalogue. Discussion group, signings. Store mascot: Jasper Bloodstone, the butler.

☞ CRIME INK

Shop 500 Upper Floor
Australia on Collins
260 Elizabeth St
Melbourne VIC 3000 AUSTRALIA

EMAIL crimeink@bigpond.com

  New crime bookstore with international mail-order service. Free monthly colour catalogue.

THE CRIME SCENE BOOKSTORE

190 Whatley Crescent
Maylands WAU 6051 AUSTRALIA

PHONE +61 8 9471 9244
EMAIL crimescn@iinet.net.au

  New and used crime fiction, with emphasis on rare & collectible, as well as imports from UK, US, & other countries. Comfortable for browsing. Will special order. "Very temperamental" bookstore cat Claude.

CRIME TIME BOOKS

Linda Bivens
1393 E Washington Blvd
Pasadena CA 91104-2533 USA

PHONE 1-626-798-2013
FAX 1-626-798-2673
EMAIL crimetimebooks@aol.com

  Est. 1996. Wide assortment of new mystery, detective & crime fiction. British imports in hardcover and paperback. Collectible first editions. Author signings. Newsletter.

☞ CRIMES INK

Nigel Piercy
35 Moreton Close
London E5 9EP ENGLAND

PHONE/FAX +44 20 8806 1895
EMAIL crimesink@q-serve.com
WEBSITE www.abebooks.com/home/
1048357/

  ☽ ✉ Detective fiction, true crime, criminology, law & police force histories.

☞ CRIMINAL PURSUITS

Elaine & Bill Kelley
5760 N Camino Padre Isidoro
Tucson AZ 85718 USA

PHONE 1-520-529-3384
EMAIL Ejkelley@aol.com

Catalog sales of modern first-edition mysteries. Also true crime, modern fiction.

CROSSHAVEN BOOKS

Eugene Gilmore
3916 Crosshaven Dr
Birmingham AL 35243-5414 USA

PHONE 1-205-972-8778
FAX 1-205-972-8779
TOLLFREE 1-888-972-8778
EMAIL crosshavenbooks@msn.com
WEBSITE www.crosshavenbooks.com

General neighborhood bookstore hosts local chapter of Sisters in Crime. Signing events. Co-sponsor of **Murder in the Magic City**. Online book sales. ABA.

CSL BOOKS

Cornell Stamoran
PO Box 297
Raritan NJ 08869 USA

PHONE 1-908-672-5665
FAX 1-888-203-5517
EMAIL sales@cslbooks.com
WEBSITE www.cslbooks.com
WEBSITE www.abebooks.com/home/ cslbooks/

Rare and collectible first editions and services to discriminating bibliophiles. Specializing in collections development in mystery, crime and detective fiction & scholarship. Mail-order/email/online, want lists welcome. ABA, IMBA, IOBA.

DANNER'S BOOKS AND COFFEE SHOP

Susan Danner
2902 W White River Blvd
Muncie IN 47304 USA

PHONE 1-765-288-1122
FAX 1-765-288-3062
EMAIL sdanner02@msn.com
WEBSITE www.dannersbooks.com

Store has all kinds of new books but primarily mystery & children's. Also does email and mail order. Newsletter. Events. Mystery book club meets monthly. Est. 1975. ABA. Shop cat Leaf.

DARK CARNIVAL

Jack Rems
3086 Claremont Ave
Berkeley CA 94705-2630 USA

PHONE 1-510-654-7323
EMAIL books@darkcarnival.com
WEBSITE www.darkcarnival.com

+ Wide selection of in-print mystery, SF, horror. Imports, juvenile & YA. Also true crime, books on death, gargoyles, unusual toys, many Edward Gorey items. Author signings. Email notices of events. NCIBA.

DAVID LENAT, BOOKSELLER

3607 Corbin St	PHONE	1-919-787-8087
Raleigh NC 27612-4601 USA	EMAIL	lenatbks@mindspring.com

Mysteries, especially Southern authors and book-related. Modern literature, especally Southern authors. Call or write for free catalogs, specify mystery or literature.

DEAD END BOOKS

	EMAIL	info@deadendbooks.com
	WEBSITE	www.deadendbooks.com

Online or email orders only. Classic and modern mystery & crime titles, mostly remainders but some first editions and used books. Will accept special orders.

DEAD WRITE BOOKS

Jill Sanagan	PHONE	1-604-228-8223
4333 #1 W 10th Ave	EMAIL	whitedwarf@deadwrite.com
Vancouver BC V6R 2H6 CANADA	WEBSITE	www.deadwrite.com

Crime & mystery. New books & audio tapes. Sister store of White Dwarf Books (fantasy & SF). Quarterly catalog of new releases.

DEADLY PASSIONS BOOKSHOP

Jim Huang, Owner	TOLLFREE	1-800-643-6737
484 E Carmel Dr #378	FAX	1-317-705-1402
Carmel IN 46032-2812 USA	EMAIL	sales@deadlypassions.com
	WEBSITE	www.deadlypassions.com

Mail/phone/internet orders only. New storefront listed under **The Mystery Company**. Mystery, SF/fantasy, romance. New and used books (mostly readers copies), some collectible. Newsletter. Want lists welcome. IMBA.

DETECTO MYSTERIOSO BOOKS

Deen Kogan	PHONE	1-215-923-0211
c/o Society Hill Playhouse	FAX	1-215-923-1789
507 S 8th St	EMAIL	shp@erols.com
Philadelphia PA 19147-1325 USA	EMAIL	DeenKogan@NovelHost.net

Mail order. Used, firsts & rare mystery & detective fiction. Sponsors **Mid-Atlantic Mystery Book Fair**. ABA, NAIBA.

THE DOCKSIDE BOOKSHOP

Havensite Mall	PHONE	1-340-774-4937
Saint Thomas VI 00802 USA		

A general bookstore with a good mystery section.

DON CANNON EPICUREAN BOOKS

10921 Chandler Blvd	PHONE	1-818-508-4735
North Hollywood CA 91601-2944	FAX	1-818-508-7230
USA	EMAIL	dcannon1@ix.netcom.com

Mail order and by appointment. Specializing in first edition mysteries, new, used, & collectible.

DONALD YATES, BOOKSELLER

555 Canon Park Dr	PHONE	1-707-963-0201
Saint Helena CA 94574-9726 USA	FAX	1-707-963-0393
	EMAIL	shsirene@aol.com

☾ ✉ Magazines, fanzines, first editions. Back issues of mystery digest magazines.

DUNN & POWELL BOOKS

Steve Powell & William Dunn	PHONE	1-207-288-4665
The Hideaway	FAX	1-603-994-7771
Bar Harbor ME 04609-1714 USA	EMAIL	dpbooks@acadia.net
	WEBSITE	www.dpbooks.com
	WEBSITE	www.abebooks.com/home/dpbooks/

☾ ✉ ⌀ Crime, mystery, detective fiction. Firsts & collectible hardbacks. Catalog available by mail or online. Online sales at ABE. Open by appointment.

EDVIGA BOOKS

John Gralinski, Proprietor	PHONE	1-607-265-9229
PO Box 286	FAX	1-607-265-9227
Masonville NY 13804-0286 USA	EMAIL	edvigabooks@citlink.net
	WEBSITE	www.edvigabooks.com

☾ ✉ ⌀ Specializes in first editions of mystery, crime, and detective fiction. Orders by phone, fax, email, or website. Website features full-size pictures of the books for sale. IMBA. Cat: Purrsa.

ELIZABETH WOLFE, BOOKSELLER

PO Box 703033	PHONE	1-972-307-5906
Dallas TX 75370-3033 USA	FAX	1-972-307-5901
	EMAIL	wolfebooks@aol.com

☾ ✉ Modern first editions, mystery & detective fiction, many signed. Mail order only. Catalog available, want lists welcome.

ELSE FINE BOOKS

Allen M Hemlock & Louise Ober-schmidt	PHONE	1-313-582-1080
	FAX	1-313-584-1591
PO Box 43	EMAIL	mail@elsefine.com
Dearborn MI 48121-0043 USA	WEBSITE	www.elsefine.com

☾ ✉ ⌀ Fine first editions, collectible & rare only. Mystery and other genres. Catalogs issued quarterly, visitors seen by appointment. Online sales through ABE and Bibliofind. ABAA, ILAB.

ELSEWHERE BOOKS

Amy Beasom, Owner	PHONE	1-415-661-2535
260 Judah St	EMAIL	elsewer@pacbell.net
San Francisco CA 94122-2404 USA		

☾ ⌂ Mysteries, SF, horror. Used & collectible hardcovers, paperbacks & magazines. Open Weds–Sun.

☞ FEMMES FATALES

Marisa Babjak	PHONE	1-562-924-6711
PO Box 3457	FAX	1-562-809-1892
Lakewood CA 90712-3457 USA	TOLLFREE	1-800-596-DEAD
	EMAIL	byteocrime@aol.com
	WEBSITE	www.mysterygifts.biz

🦅 ✉ ⌀ All mystery titles, writing and crime references, underground publications, foreign language Sherlock Holmes books. Canadian, Australian, British mystery titles. Some out of print and first editions of American authors.

FICKES CRIME FICTION

Patricia A Fickes	PHONE	1-330-773-4223
1471 Burkhardt Ave	FAX	1-330-773-4235
Akron OH 44301-2305 USA	EMAIL	fickes@apk.net

☾ ✉ Mail order or email. Catalog of used, rare, and first editions.

THE FINE BOOKS COMPANY

David & Nancy Aronovitz	PHONE	1-248-651-8799
781 E Snell Rd	FAX	1-248-651-6542
Rochester MI 48306-2144 USA	EMAIL	finebook@mich.com
	WEBSITE	www.abebooks.com/home/finebook/
	WEBSITE	www.mich.com/~finebook/

☾ ✉ ⌀ Rare & first editions, manuscripts, books, periodicals. Literature, SF/fantasy, children's & illustrated, as well as mystery/detective fiction. Mail order, online, or by appointment. ABE website has all books; mich.com website has latest catalog. Print catalogs available. ABAA.

FOUL PLAY MYSTERY BOOKSHOP

John & Toni Cross	PHONE	1-614-818-CLUE
27 E College Ave	EMAIL	foulplaybk@aol.com
Westerville OH 43081-2101 USA	WEBSITE	www.foulplaybooks.com

🦅 🏚 ♿ Both new and used mysteries, with stickers identifying them as cozies, private eyes, spies, etc. Want lists welcome. Shop is an old Victorian house. ABA, Book Sense. Cats are Fannie and Desiree.

FRANK S POLLACK

1214 Green Bay Rd	PHONE	1-847-433-2213
Highland Park IL 60035-4011 USA	FAX	1-312-372-8343
	EMAIL	fpollack@compuserve.com

☾ ✉ First edition mystery & detective fiction, modern literature. Catalog, searches. Mail order or by appointment.

FULL CIRCLE BOOKSTORE

Connie Heppner, Mystery Buyer	PHONE	1-405-842-2900
50 Penn Place	TOLLFREE	1-800-683-READ
1900 NW Expressway St Ste 302R	EMAIL	fullcirclebooks@aol.com
Oklahoma City OK 73118-1808		
USA		

☼ ⌂ Very large store with active mystery program, events & signings. ABA.

☛ G CURWEN BOOKS

Ginger Curwen & Jack Nessel	PHONE	1-212-595-5904
1 W 67th St #710	EMAIL	gcbks@earthlink.net
New York NY 10023 USA	WEBSITE	www.abebooks.com/home/gcbks/

☾ ⌀ Mysteries, literary firsts, magic. Catalogs issued, want lists welcomed.

GALLERY BOOKSHOP

Tony Miksak, Owner	PHONE	1-707-937-BOOK
319 Kasten St	FAX	1-707-937-3737
PO Box 270	EMAIL	info@gallerybooks.com
Mendocino CA 95460-0270 USA	WEBSITE	www.gallerybooks.com

☼ ⌂ General bookstore with large mystery collection. Signings & readers groups. Will do out-of-print searches. ABA, NCIBA. Bookstore cat: Colette.

GARDEN DISTRICT BOOK SHOP

Britton Trice, Owner	PHONE	1-504-895-2266
2727 Prytania St	FAX	1-504-895-0111
New Orleans LA 70130-5968 USA	EMAIL	betbooks@aol.com

☼ ⌂ ♿ ✉ Hosts signings. New, used, collectible books. Newsletter. Also does mail order. ABA.

GASLIGHT BOOKS

Gayle & Robert Lovett	PHONE/FAX	+61 2 6239 3633
Unit 10, 83 Wollongong St	EMAIL	gasbooks@gaslightbooks.com.au
(PO Box 267)	WEBSITE	www.gaslightbooks.com.au
Fyshwick ACT 2609 AUSTRALIA		

☙+ ⌂ ✉ Crime & detective fiction, science fiction, fantasy, horror. New and used, Australian, UK, and US editions. Catalog on web site, want lists welcome. Will ship overseas.

GEIGER'S BOOKS

Gary Decker	PHONE	1-831-335-5870
PO Box 66223	EMAIL	books@baymoon.com
Scotts Valley CA 95067-6223 USA	WEBSITE	www.geigers.com

☾ ✉ California & the West, literature, mystery/detective fiction. Firsts & collectible.

GEORGE EASTER, BOOKSELLER

PO Box 969	PHONE	1-801-294-7232
Bountiful UT 84011-0969 USA	FAX	1-801-296-1993
	WEBSITE	www.deadlypleasures.com/
		BooksForSaleMaster.htm
	EMAIL	george@deadlypleasures.com

UK and US hardcovers. Many books listed at website are linked to reviews from *Deadly Pleasures* magazine. Additional stock listed at ABE.

GORGON BOOKS

21 Deer Lane	PHONE	1-516-781-0439
Wantagh NY 11793 USA	EMAIL	bookman318@yahoo.com
	WEBSITE	gorgon.hypermart.net

Specializing in signed hardcover first editions. Also carries audiobooks and sets of paperbacks by your favorite authors.

GRAVE MATTERS

Alice Ann Carpenter & John Leini-	PHONE	1-513-242-7527
nger	FAX	1-513-242-5115
PO Box 32192	TOLLFREE	1-800-491-3741
Cincinnati OH 45232-0192 USA	EMAIL	books@gravematters.com
	WEBSITE	www.gravematters.com

Mail order & secure online ordering. Firsts (new and used), vintage, reference, Sherlockiana, magazines, reading copies. Monthly catalog online or by mail. Est. 1986. IMBA. Cats Diablo, Elmo, & Mystery.

GRAVESEND BOOKS

Enola Stewart	PHONE	1-570-646-3317
PO Box 235	EMAIL	gravesnd@epix.net
Pocono Pines PA 18350-0235 USA		

Annotated catalogs for librarians & serious collectors—exceptionally informative. Specializes in Sherlockiana & analytical material. Used, firsts, rare.

GREEN LION BOOKS

Mark Goodman, Manager	PHONE	1-651-644-9070
2402 University Ave W #409		
Saint Paul MN 55114-1701 USA		

Mail order or by appointment. Large selection of used, firsts, rare. General fiction, tough guy & crime, SF, westerns, movie/TV tie-ins, vintage paperbacks. Want lists welcome, free search service.

GREENWOODS BOOKSHOPPE

Barry Hammond	PHONE	1-780-439-2005
10355 Whyte Ave	FAX	1-780-433-5774
Edmonton AB T6E 1Z9 CANADA	TOLLFREE	1-800-661-2078
	EMAIL	books@greenwoods.com
	WEBSITE	www.greenwoods.com

☼ ⌂ Large independent bookshop includes some enthusiastic mystery fans on staff. Reviews & recommendations at website.

☛ GRYPHON BOOKS

Gary Lovisi	PHONE	1-718-646-6126
PO Box 209	EMAIL	orders@gryphonbooks.com
Brooklyn NY 11228-0209 USA	WEBSITE	www.gryphonbooks.com

☾ ✉ Specializing in genre paperbacks and pulps. Online catalog.

HAMMETT KRIMIBUCHHANDLUNG

Friesenstrasse 27	PHONE	+49 30 691 58 34
10965 Berlin GERMANY	FAX	+49 30 693 35 65
	EMAIL	hammett@hammett-krimis.de
	WEBSITE	www.hammett-krimis.de

🦅 ⌂ Small crime fiction bookstore with active website: catalog, sales, bulletin board, links. New & used, many titles in English.

HARD BOILED NOIR BOOKS

Raymond Garcia	PHONE	1-517-337-7597
204 S Clippert	EMAIL	garciara@msu.edu
Lansing MI 48912 USA	WEBSITE	www.abebooks.com/home/ hbnbooks/

☾ ⌀ Hard-boiled detectives, mean streets stories, dark tales of life in an incoherent or oppressive world, and mysteries of all kinds.

THE HAUNT

Glenn Grant, Owner	PHONE	1-808-943-0371
2634 S King St #3	FAX	1-808-951-8878
Honolulu HI 96826-3243 USA	EMAIL	timewalks@pixi.com
	WEBSITE	www.chicken-skin.com

🦅+ ⌂ Hawaii's first mystery bookstore, specializing in supernatural, hardboiled mystery, and Hawaiian history. Events, poetry, music.

HAWKLINE BOOKS

Jeff Kunkle & Kelly Burg	PHONE	1-503-233-5193
PO Box 42602	EMAIL	hawkline@teleport.com
Portland OR 97242-0602 USA	WEBSITE	www.teleport.com/~hawkline/

☾ ✉ ⌀ Fine first editions with an emphasis on mystery. Email or phone orders. Selected catalog online, also at ABE.

Heisey Hasbeens

Toni Heisey   PHONE   1-530-253-3433
PO Box 1177
Janesville CA 96114-1177 USA

General with mystery emphasis. Modern firsts, horror, Doc Savage & philatelic. Catalog available.

High Crimes

Cynthia Nye, Owner	PHONE	1-303-443-8346
946 Pearl St	FAX	1-303-443-1818
Boulder CO 80302-5109 USA	TOLLFREE	1-800-356-5586
	EMAIL	highcrimes@earthlink.net
	WEBSITE	www.highcrimesbooks.com

British imports featured in extensive stock of new mysteries. Publishes *The Purloined Letter* newsletter. ABA, IMBA.

Horizon West Books

Lester Elisco	PHONE	1-818-554-9873
2222 Foothill Blvd Ste E-217	EMAIL	MrEsbooks@aol.com
La Cañada CA 91011-1498 USA	WEBSITE	www.abebooks.com/home/ horizonwest/

Mostly used, some new, specializing in hardcover, first edition, detective fiction, also SF and general fiction. Online catalog at ABE and TomFolio.

I Love a Mystery (Mission KS)

Karen Spengler, Owner	PHONE	1-913-432-2583
5460 Martway St	TOLLFREE	1-877-474-2583
Mission KS 66205-2915 USA	EMAIL	kas@iloveamystery.net

New, used & out-of-print mysteries. Cozies to hardboiled, paperbacks & hardbacks. Signed first editions. Bimonthly newsletter by subscription. Email notification of store events. IMBA, ABA.

I Love a Mystery (Slingerlands NY)

William L Simmons, Owner	PHONE	1-518-439-6782
1621 New Scotland Rd	EMAIL	bilams@nycap.rr.com
Slingerlands NY 12159-9239 USA	WEBSITE	www.abebooks.com/home/ilam/

Mail order only. Used, rare, and firsts. Specializing in mystery & related genre. Catalogs issued irregularly. Books listed on ABE.

It's a Mystery Bookstore (Saskatoon SK)

Isabel Jungwirth	PHONE/FAX	1-306-384-6464
527 Main St	EMAIL	mysterybooks@sk.sympatico.ca
Saskatoon SK S7N 0C2 CANADA	WEBSITE	www.abebooks.com/home/ itsamystery

Small store packed with new & used mystery & detective fiction, a few reference & true crime. Mystery puzzles, cassette tapes, *Mystery Review* magazine. Email and mail orders, online sales through ABE. CBA.

☛ It's a Mystery to Me (Yeadon, PA)

723 Church Lane	PHONE	1-610-623-1006
Yeadon PA 19050-3502 USA	FAX	1-610-623-1166

🦅 🏛 African-American intrigue, suspense and mysteries—providing a soulful salute to African-American fiction and its counterparts. ABA.

J Jay Johnson, Bookseller

	EMAIL	jjayj@erols.com
	WEBSITE	www.abebooks.com/home/jjayj/

☽ ∅ Collector and dealer specializing in signed first editions, mysteries, SF, fantasy. Email/online only, sends advance catalogs by email. Want lists welcome.

James Pepper Rare Books

2026 Cliff Dr Ste 224	PHONE	1-805-963-1025
Santa Barbara CA 93109-1593 USA	FAX	1-805-966-9737
	EMAIL	pepbooks@aol.com
	WEBSITE	abaa.org/pepper/

☽ ✉ ∅ Collectible & rare mystery & detective, literature, cinema. Catalog available. Online sales at ABE. Open by appointment only. ABAA.

Jamie Fraser Books

427A Queen St W, 2nd fl	PHONE	1-416-598-7718
Toronto ON M5V 2A5 Canada	EMAIL	fraserj@interlog.com
	WEBSITE	www.interlog.com/~fraserj

☽ 🏛 ✉ ∅ Mystery & detective fiction, fantasy, horror, paperback originals, pulp magazines. Modern first, used, rare, reading copies, h/c & p/b. Shop open daily. Mail order & want lists welcome. ABAC, ILAB.

Jane Addams Book Shop

Flora Faraci, Owner	PHONE	1-217-356-2555
208 N Neil St	EMAIL	FFaraci@aol.com
Champaign IL 61820-4013 USA		

☼ 🏛 Used, firsts & rare. Mystery room with 3,000 titles. Signings, mystery newsletter. Open daily.

Janus Books

Michael S Greenbaum	PHONE	1-520-881-8192
PO Box 40787-DD	FAX	1-815-333-2938
Tucson AZ 85717-0787 USA	VOICEMAIL	1-800-986-1165
	EMAIL	mike@janusbooks.com
	WEBSITE	www.janusbooks.com

☽ ✉ Fine & first editions of Sherlock Holmes parodies & pastiches, Writings about the Writings and Arthur Conan Doyle; detective, mystery, & suspense fiction; related bibliography & criticism. Mail order/online catalog & sales. Email lists available. IOBA.

JEFFREY MEYERSON MYSTERY BOOKS

8801 Shore Rd #6A - East	PHONE	1-718-833-8248
Brooklyn NY 11209-5450 USA	EMAIL	jjmeyerson@aol.com

◖ ✉ Regular catalogs of secondhand, reasonably-priced mysteries, specializing in British publications, from reading copies to (some) collectible. Mail order only. Want lists welcome.

☞ JOHN K KING USED & RARE BOOKS

901 W Lafayette Blvd	EMAIL	kingbooks@aol.com
Detroit MI 48226 USA	WEBSITE	www.rarebooklink.com

◖ 🏬 Over a million books, in an old factory building in downtown Detroit. Well organized, well lighted, and helpful employees.

JOHN W KNOTT JR, BOOKSELLER

John & Susan Knott	PHONE/FAX	1-301-317-8427
8453 Early Bud Way	EMAIL	jwkbooks@jwkbooks.com
Laurel MD 20723-1085 USA	WEBSITE	www.abebooks.com/home/katkel/

◖ ✉ ∅ Mystery & detective first editions, vintage paperbacks, also SF, fantasy, horror, adventure. Catalogs issued. Mail order & by appointment only.

JOSEPH-BETH BOOKSELLERS (CINCINNATI OH)

Amy Fogelson	PHONE	1-513-396-8960
2692 Madison Rd	FAX	1-513-396-8975
Cincinnati OH 45208-1320 USA	TOLLFREE	1-800-396-8960
	EMAIL	info@josephbeth.com
	WEBSITE	www.josephbeth.com

☼ 🏬 Large regional independent bookstore. Readers groups, author events. Email newsletter. Special orders welcome. ABA.

JOSEPH-BETH BOOKSELLERS (CLEVELAND OH)

13217 Shaker Sq	PHONE	1-216-751-3300
Cleveland OH 44120 USA	FAX	1-216-416-4422
	EMAIL	info@josephbeth.com
	WEBSITE	www.josephbeth.com

☼ 🏬 Large regional independent bookstore. Readers groups, author events. Email newsletter. Special orders welcome. ABA.

JOSEPH-BETH BOOKSELLERS (LEXINGTON KY)

161 Lexington Green Cir Ste B1	PHONE	1-606-273-2911
Lexington KY 40503-3323 USA	FAX	1-606-272-6948
	TOLLFREE	1-800-248-6849
	EMAIL	info@josephbeth.com
	WEBSITE	www.josephbeth.com

☼ 🏬 Large regional independent bookstore. Readers groups, author events. Email newsletter. Special orders welcome. ABA.

JUST BOOKS

Jenny & Thomas Lawton
19 E Putnam Ave
Greenwich CT 06830-5443 USA

PHONE 1-203-869-5023
FAX 1-203-869-0633
TOLLFREE 1-800-874-4568
EMAIL bookshop@justbooks.org
WEBSITE www.justbook.com

☼ 🏛 ⊘ Small store but happy to special-order with quick turnaround. Author events, including meet-the-author breakfasts. Online catalog & sales. Monthly newsletter. ABA, Book Sense.

KATE'S MYSTERY BOOKS

Kate Mattes, Owner
2211 Massachusetts Ave
Cambridge MA 02140-1211 USA

PHONE 1-617-491-2660
EMAIL katesmysbks@earthlink.net
WEBSITE www.katesmysterybooks.com

🦅 🏛 Full service mystery bookstore with active readers groups. MWA & SinC meet here. New, used, firsts, rare, autographed books, plus gifts, signings, newsletter. Stock includes true crime and reference books. Want lists welcome. IMBA, NEBA.

KAYO BOOKS

Ron Blum
814 Post St
San Francisco CA 94109-6013 USA

PHONE 1-415-749-0554
EMAIL kayo@kayobooks.com
WEBSITE www.kayobooks.com

🦅 🏛 Vintage hardboiled, paperbacks, other pulp genres, related reference & ephemera. Spacious store. Want lists welcome.

KEN HEBENSTREIT, BOOKSELLER

Ken Hebenstreit & Shar Douglas,
   Owners
813 N Washington Ave
Royal Oak MI 48067-1737 USA

PHONE 1-248-548-5460
EMAIL ken@khbooks.com
WEBSITE www.khbooks.com

🦅 ✉ ⊘ First editions of contemporary fiction, mystery, suspense. Mail order; online sales at ABE, Alibris, and Bibliofind. Visitors by appointment only. Print catalog three times/year. Has the best return policy in the business. Dogs Zelda & Bagpipe.

KILL CITY CRIME BOOKS

David Pepperell, Manager
226 Chapel Street
Prahran VIC 3181 AUSTRALIA

PHONE +61 3 9510 6661
FAX +61 3 9521 4046
EMAIL killbks@ozemail.com.au

🦅 🏛 ♿ Mystery and crime fiction plus true crime, new and secondhand. Australia's first specialty crime bookstore. Est. 1992.

KILLING TIME IN KANSAS

Shari Berl-Bikson & Bruce Bikson
14033 Hayes St
Overland Park KS 66221-2014 USA

PHONE 1-913-897-7916
FAX 1-913-894-6001
EMAIL bbikson@cs.com

🦅 ✉ Mysteries, general fiction, military history. Used, firsts, rare. Mail order only.

THE KING'S ENGLISH BOOKSHOP

Betsy Burton, Owner
1511 South 1500 East
Salt Lake City UT 84105-2896 USA

PHONE 1-801-484-9100
FAX 1-801-484-1595
TOLLFREE 1-800-658-7928
EMAIL books@kingsenglish.com
WEBSITE www.kingsenglish.com

☼ 🏠 Specializes in fiction with a large mystery room & regular signings. Newsletter, *The Inkslinger*. ABA, Book Sense.

KRIMIBUCHHANDLUNG ALIBI

Barbara & Manfred Sarrazin
Ehrenstrasse 96-98
50672 Köln GERMANY

PHONE/FAX +49 221 244 496

🦅 🏠 Germany's second oldest crime bookstore, est. 1990.

KRIMIBUCHHANDLUNG GLATTEIS

Gabriele Fauser & Monika Dobler,
   Owners
Corneliusstr. 31 (Ecke Baaderstrasse)
80469 München GERMANY

PHONE +49 80 201 4844
EMAIL glatteis.krimi@t-online.de
EMAIL info@glatteis.de

🦅 🏠 Opened Sep 2000. Meetings and author readings monthly.

KRIMIS & KONSORTEN

Weidenallee 60
20357 Hamburg GERMANY

PHONE +49 40 459 254
FAX +49 40 459 259

🦅 🏠 Crime novels and companions. New books.

krimiTHEK KRIMIBIBLIOTHEK

Renate Bösch-Hess & Verena Jacot
Im Gemeinschaftszentrum Schind-
   lergut
Kronenstrasse 12
8006 Zürich SWITZERLAND

EMAIL info@krimithek.ch
WEBSITE www.krimithek.ch

🦅 🏠 Crime books in German, French, Italian, Spanish, Finnish, and Russian.

THE LAST GOOD BOOK

Louis Cristantiello
1074 Drewville Rd
Brewster NY 10509-2516 USA

PHONE 1-845-278-9332
FAX 1-845-278-6316
EMAIL lcrist6956@aol.com

🦅 ✉ New and used books by mail order. Collectible first edition mystery & detective fiction. Catalogs issued. Want lists welcome. IMBA, IOBA.

LAST SEEN READING

Bonnie & David Pollard	PHONE	1-650-321-3348
PO Box 1423	EMAIL	dpollard@slip.net
Palo Alto CA 94302-1423 USA		

Out of print mysteries (h/c & p/b) , juvenile fiction, and fibercrafts. Some books by English novelists and miscellaneous fiction and nonfiction. Occasional catalogs. Want lists accepted. Cat named Toby.

LATIN BLOOD BOOKS

Dale Carter	PHONE/FAX	1-818-344-1613
PO Box 7733	EMAIL	dv.carter@att.net
Van Nuys CA 91409-7733 USA	WEBSITE	dogbert.abebooks.com/abe/Client Home?clientId=848233

Signed first editions (both new and used) of mystery & detective fiction, Latin American literature, & modern fiction.

LEATHER STALKING BOOKS

Bill & Vi Elsey	PHONE	1-607-547-5748
107 Bartlett Rd	TOLLFREE	1-888-563-2244
Cooperstown NY 13326-3318 USA	EMAIL	elseybks@telenet.net
	WEBSITE	www.leatherstalkingbooks.com

Fine first editions, specializing in mystery & detective fiction. Catalogs issued, searches, appraisals. Open Wed–Sat, June 1–Labor Day; otherwise by appointment or chance. Online & mail order anytime. Want lists welcome. IOBA.

LEFT FOR DEAD BOOKS

Kevin Murnane, Owner	PHONE	1-301-277-3964
4021 Beechwood Rd	FAX	1-301-277-3462
University Park MD 20782-1429	EMAIL	mysteries@leftfordeadbooks.com
USA	WEBSITE	www.leftfordeadbooks.com

Specializing in first editions of mystery and crime fiction, fantasy and science fiction. Will buy collections large and small. Mail order; online sales through ABE, Bibliofind. Want lists welcome. Biweekly email catalog.

LEGENDS FINE & RARE BOOKS

Robert & Michael DeSarro	PHONE	1-909-868-0997
196 Garfield Ave	FAX	1-909-868-0754
Pomona CA 91767 USA	TOLLFREE	1-866-350-6100
	EMAIL	mail@legendsbooks.com
	WEBSITE	www.legendsbooks.com

Modern US & UK first editions. Mystery, horror, adventure, modern literature. Monthly magazine, *Storyteller,* available by mail. Also auctions at Ebay. ABAA, ILAB.

LEN UNGER—RARE BOOKS

Len & Toby Unger	PHONE	1-818-990-7569
PO Box 5858	FAX	1-818-905-7909
Sherman Oaks CA 91413-5858 USA	EMAIL	lenunger@msn.com
	WEBSITE	abaa.org/usa/len.unger/
	WEBSITE	www.abebooks.com/home/ lenunger/

☾ ✉ ⊘ Mystery & detective fiction, westerns. Modern firsts & rare. Catalog available. Online sales through ABE. ABAA.

LIBRERIA SUSPENSE

Via Ceresio 87/89	PHONE	+39 6 8535 8291
00199 Roma ITALY	EMAIL	suspense@tin.it
	EMAIL	suspense@tiscalinet.it
	EMAIL	suspense@infinito.it

🦅 🏛 New and used books: noir, spy story, horror, fantasy, and more. Also conducts "Mystery Tours" of the most mysterious places in Rome.

THE LITERATE TRAVELLER

Nancy Heck	PHONE	1-310-313-2453
8306 Wilshire Blvd #591	FAX	1-310-313-6894
Beverly Hills CA 90211-2382 USA	TOLLFREE	1-800-850-2665
	EMAIL	literate@cyberjava.com
	WEBSITE	www.literatetraveller.com

☼ ✉ Mail order only. Website features "Around the World in 80 Mysteries," a selection of English-language mystery books in international settings, as well as a full range of travel books. Annual print catalog. ABA.

☞ LITTLE HOUSE MYSTERIES

| 204 Cullum Ave | EMAIL | clymer3285@aol.com |
| Dickson TN 37055 USA | WEBSITE | www.auntb3285.mybravenet.com |

☾ ✉ Used and out-of-print. Online sales through Amazon Marketplace and zShops.

LOOMPANICS UNLIMITED

Michael Hoy, President	PHONE	1-360-385-2230
PO Box 1197	FAX	1-360-385-7785
Port Townsend WA 98368-0997 USA	TOLLFREE	1-800-380-2230
	EMAIL	service@loompanics.com
	WEBSITE	www.loompanics.com

☼ ✉ ⊘ Non-fiction only. Publisher and distributor of unusual & controversial how-to and reference books. Wide range of crime-writing-related subjects (e.g. lock-picking, wiretapping, poisons) as well as self-help and survival literature. Excellent resource for writers. Catalog online or $5 (free with purchase); includes articles & features.

"M" Is For Mystery

Ed & Jeannie Kaufman, Owners
86 E 3rd Ave
San Mateo CA 94401-4011 USA

PHONE 1-650-401-8077
FAX 1-650-401-8079
TOLLFREE 1-888-405-8077
EMAIL info@MforMystery.com
WEBSITE www.MforMystery.com

New, first & limited editions, used. Audio & gifts. Signings, reading club, newsletter. Weekly e-newsletter free on request. IMBA, ABA, NCIBA.

Mad 4 Mysteries

Maddy van Hertbruggen
12711 Orchard Hollow Way
Houston TX 77065 USA

EMAIL maddyvan@att.net

First edition mysteries. Online sales at ABE.

Magna Mysteries

Gordon A Magnuson
PO Box 5732
Virginia Beach VA 23471-0732 USA

PHONE 1-757-464-5861
FAX 1-757-464-0254
EMAIL magnamys@pilot.infi.net

Detective fiction. Used, firsts & rare.

Mail Order Mysteries/ Ann Arbor Books Online

Judith Anne Steeh
1313 Henry St
Ann Arbor MI 48104-4405 USA

PHONE 1-734-665-5813
FAX 1-734-665-7775
EMAIL A2Mystery@aol.com

Used, firsts, out of print for readers and collectors. Mail order, email, online.

Mainly Murder Bookstore

Patricia Barry, Owner
2a Paul St
Cork IRELAND

PHONE/FAX +353 21 427 2413

First bookstore in Ireland to specialize in crime fiction, true crime & detection.

Malice, The Mystery Bookstore

Carolyn C Clement
346 NW Bond St
Bend OR 97701 USA

PHONE 1-541-388-3238
EMAIL alice@malicebooks.com
WEBSITE www.malicebooks.com

Selling reviewed and recommended new books by mail, handpicked by "Alice Malice," a bookseller for 20 years. Online catalog organized by subgenre. IMBA, ABA.

Maple Street Book Store

7523 Maple St
New Orleans LA 70118-5098 USA

PHONE 1-504-866-4916
EMAIL rhoda@maplestreetbookshop.com
WEBSITE www.maplestreetbookshop.com

Staffed by bibliophiles. Hosts signings. Newsletter. ABA.

MARY MASON, BOOKSELLER

PO Box 15804	PHONE	1-619-287-2299
San Diego CA 92175-5804 USA	EMAIL	maggiemary@yahoo.com

Mail order or by appointment. New & used, signed books, mainly mystery, unique cookbooks, & children's. Fan guest of honor at Bouchercon 1999. IMBA.

McCOY'S RARE BOOKS

Jamie & Patti McCoy	PHONE	1-908-713-6720
21 Austin Hill Rd	FAX	1-908-713-6730
Clinton NJ 08809-2038 USA	EMAIL	mccoybks@earthlink.net
	WEBSITE	www.mccoysbooks.com

Internet & mail order or by appointment. For serious collectors of mystery, SF, & modern literature. Want lists accepted.

McINTYRE'S FINE BOOKS & BOOKENDS

Robert Segedy, Buyer	PHONE	1-919-542-3030
2000 Fearrington Village Ctr	FAX	1-919-542-5196
Pittsboro NC 27312-8502 USA	EMAIL	books@fearrington.com
	WEBSITE	www.fearrington.com/McIntyres/mcintyres.html

Friendly independent bookstore with excellent mystery section. Numerous signings. Electronic newsletter twice a month; send email to sign up. Will ship in US. ABA, Book Sense.

MECHANICSBURG MYSTERY BOOK SHOP

Deborah Beamer	PHONE	1-717-795-7470
6 Clouser Rd	FAX	1-717-795-7473
Mechanicsburg PA 17055-9735 USA	EMAIL	beamerpa@epix.net

Mostly new books, some used, a few rare. ABA.

MICHEL LANTEIGNE—BOOKSELLER

5468 Rue St Urbain #4	PHONE	1-514-273-4963
Montreal PQ H2T 2X1 CANADA	EMAIL	mlb@securenet.net
	WEBSITE	www.abebooks.com/home/michellanteigne/

Mail order and online sales only. Collectible crime & mystery first editions, out-of-print, rare, Sherlockiana, vintage paperbacks.

MIKE'S EVIL DEEDS

Michael Lange	PHONE	1-617-332-6269
170 Auburn St	EMAIL	evildeed@ziplink.net
Auburndale MA 02466-2412 USA		

Mystery & detective fiction, 1890s to 1970s. Collectible firsts & quality reprints. Mail order only. Want lists welcome. Free catalogs.

MING BOOKS

Marion & Robin Richmond	PHONE	+44 1988 402653
Beechwood, Acre Place	EMAIL	info@mingbooks.com
Wigtown, Newton Stewart DG8 9DU	EMAIL	mingbooks@supanet.com
SCOTLAND	WEBSITE	www.mingbooks.com
	WEBSITE	www.mingbooks.co.uk

☾ ✉ ∅ Large stock of used mystery, crime, suspense, espionage & detective fiction. Also true crime and true espionage. Hardback, paperback, for readers and collectors. Open daily in summer; winter by appt. Online sales through ABE & BookAvenue. Want lists very welcome. Catalogues issued.

MISSING LINK: ZWEIGNIEDERLASSUNG BONN

Thomas Przybilka	PHONE	+49 228 24 21 383
Buschstrasse 14	FAX	+49 228 24 21 385
53113 Bonn GERMANY	EMAIL	mlbonn@t-online.de

☾ ✉ Specialist in international secondary literature related to crime & mystery fiction. Mail order, new books. Newsletter *Krimi-Tipp.*

MisterE BOOKS AND RECORDS

Ed Leimbacher	PHONE	1-206-463-3973
PO Box 2149	EMAIL	mistere@mistere.com
Vashon WA 98070 USA	WEBSITE	www.mistere.com

☾ ✉ ∅ Shop closed, now mail-order/online only. Mysteries, graphic novels, children's and illustrated, vintage vinyl. Online sales through ABE.

MITCHELL BOOKS

John Mitchell	PHONE	1-626-798-4438
1395 E Washington Blvd	FAX	1-626-798-0100
Pasadena CA 91104-2533 USA	EMAIL	mb4mystery@aol.com
	WEBSITE	www.mysteryfiction.com

☾ 🏛 ∅ Mystery, detective, crime, and spy fiction; used and collectible only. Specialties pre-1945, women authors, hardboiled, reference & periodicals. Large stock, want lists welcome. Online sales at website.

MOBY DICKENS BOOKSHOP

Art & Susan Bachrach, Owners	PHONE	1-505-758-3050
124A Bent St	FAX	1-505-758-9391
Taos NM 87571-5992 USA	TOLLFREE	1-888-442-9980
	EMAIL	mobyop@newmex.com
	WEBSITE	www.mobydickens.com

☼ 🏛 "Who Did It? A Grammatically Correct Mystery Book Club" hosts writers and introduces members to new authors. New, out-of-print and rare books. Extensive children's & young adult mystery sections. Newsletter and bibliography of New Mexico mystery writers at website.

MONROE STAHR BOOKS

Tom Rusch	PHONE	1-818-501-3419
5112 Van Noord Ave	FAX	1-866-728-1119
Sherman Oaks CA 91423-1664 USA	EMAIL	MStahrBks@aol.com
	WEBSITE	www.abebooks.com/home/ monroestahrbks/

 ☏ ✉ ∅ Mail order and by appointment. Catalogs. Collectible and first edition detective fiction, the Hollywood novel & surfing.

MORD & TOTSCHLAG

Karl-Marx-Str. 6	PHONE	+49 531 707 5520
38104 Braunschweig GERMANY	EMAIL	thiemig@direct-line.de

 ☏ Murder & Homicide. Krimi-Antiquariat.

MORDIDA BOOKS

Dick Wilson	PHONE	1-713-467-4280
PO Box 79322	FAX	1-713-467-4182
Houston TX 77279-9322 USA	EMAIL	mordida@swbell.net
	WEBSITE	www.mordida.com

 ☏ ✉ Fine first editions and rare mystery & detective fiction, from the 19th century to the Golden Age to hypermoderns.

MOSTLY MURDER, MYSTERY & MAYHEM (SOUTH GRAFTON, MA)

Marshall W Snow	PHONE/FAX	1-508-839-3241
292 Providence Rd	EMAIL	mmmmsnow@aol.com
South Grafton MA 01560-1337 USA	WEBSITE	www.mostly-murder.com

 ☏ ✉ ∅ Mail order. Online sales at ABE. Also publishes annually *The Comprehensive Price Guide of Crime, Mystery, Thriller, Detective and Horror Fiction.*

MOSTLY MYSTERIES (LEAWOOD KS)

Randy MacPherson	PHONE	1-913-402-9599
4813 W 148th St	EMAIL	mostlymyst@aol.com
Leawood KS 66224 USA		

 ☏ ✉ First editions, many signed. Catalog available. Mail order & by appt.

☛ MOSTLY MYSTERIES (NASHVILLE TN)

Kathy Emery	PHONE	1-615-298-1436
4800 Nevada Ave	EMAIL	kemerytn@yahoo.com
Nashville TN 37209 USA	WEBSITE	www.abebooks.com/home/ mmmbooks/

 ☏ ∅ Used hardback & paperback mysteries. Online at ABE.

MOSTLY MYSTERY (ARCHBALD PA)

Ed McDonald	PHONE	1-570-876-2783
PO Box 52		
Archbald PA 18403-0052 USA		

 ☏ ✉ Mystery & detective fiction. Used, firsts & rare. Hardcover & vintage paperback. Catalog available.

MOUNTAIN MYSTERIES

Jim & Kathleen Wood
PO Box 14158
Bradenton FL 34280-4158 USA

PHONE 1-941-761-9044
FAX 1-941-792-5712
EMAIL mtmystery@aol.com
WEBSITE dogbert.abebooks.com/abe/ClientHome?clientId=863947

⟨ ✉ ∅ Used mysteries: "Collector's copies, reading copies & everything in between." Hardcovers. Mail order, open by appointment. Quarterly catalogs. IMBA.

MURDER A LA CARTE BOOKS

Barbara J Kincaid
PO Box 995
Great Falls VA 22066-0995 USA

PHONE 1-703-450-1112
FAX 1-703-450-7581
EMAIL bjkincaid@cox.net
WEBSITE www.abebooks.com/home/fallingwater/

⟨ ✉ ∅ Specializing in Doubleday Crime Club 1928-1991. Emphasis on mystery, detective, military, adventure, signed modern fiction, and a little of everything.

☛ MURDER AND MAYHEM

5 Lion Street
Hay-on-Wye, Hereford HR3 5AA
WALES

EMAIL madness@hay-on-wyebooks.com
WEBSITE www.hay-on-wyebooks.com

⟨ ⌂ ∅ Detective fiction, true crime, and some horror. Online sales via abebooks.com.

MURDER BY THE BOOK (CRANSTON RI)

Kevin J Barbero, Owner
1645 Warwick Ave Ste 202
Warwick RI 02889-1524 USA

PHONE 1-401-739-7224
EMAIL kbbooks1@cox.net
WEBSITE www.abebooks.com/home/kbbooks/

🦉 ✉ ∅ Mail order, online at ABE. Mystery, thrillers, detective, and spy novels. Firsts, used, rare, some new. British imports. Visitors welcome by appointment.

MURDER BY THE BOOK (DENVER CO)

Lauri Verschure & Joan D Montgomery
1574 S Pearl St
Denver CO 80210-2635 USA

PHONE 1-303-871-9401
FAX 1-303-871-8253
TOLLFREE 1-800-300-2595
EMAIL info@murderbythebook.com
WEBSITE www.murderbythebook.com

🦉 ⌂ Full service mystery bookstore with large selection. New books, collectible, used. Signings & events. IMBA.

MURDER BY THE BOOK (HOUSTON TX)

Martha Farrington, Owner	PHONE	1-713-524-8597
Dean James, Manager	FAX	1-713-522-7945
2342 Bissonnet St	TOLLFREE	1-888-4AGATHA
Houston TX 77005-1512 USA	EMAIL	murderbk@swbell.net
	WEBSITE	www.murderbooks.com

New, used, firsts & rare. Gifts, reading group, signings, online sales. Quarterly magazine *The Dead Beat.* Want lists welcome. ABA, IMBA. Bookstore dogs: Archie Goodwin & Lily Rowan.

MURDER BY THE BOOK (PORTLAND OR)

Jill Hinckley & Carolyn Lane	PHONE	1-503-232-9995
3210 SE Hawthorne Blvd	FAX	1-503-232-2554
Portland OR 97214-5045 USA	EMAIL	books@mbtb.com
	WEBSITE	www.mbtb.com

New, used & rare, hardcover & paperback, mystery & related genres. Gifts, audio books, videos. Open daily, or order online. Occasional newsletter *Murder by the Bye.* Want lists welcome, and wish list gift registry kept. Est. 1983. IMBA.

MURDER FOR FUN BOOKSHOP

Pat O'Keefe, Owner	PHONE	1-919-469-9473
2115 W Marilyn Cir		
Cary NC 27513-5302 USA		

By mail only. New hard & softcovers but will happily search for used.

MURDER IN PRINT

Steve & Barbara Strange	PHONE	1-817-429-8899
3602 Ivywild Ct	FAX	1-817-457-5055
Arlington TX 76016-3044 USA	EMAIL	murderinprint@swbell.net
	WEBSITE	www.abebooks.com/home/191789/

Mail order and online only. Mystery & detective fiction, SF, pulps, vintage paperbacks, and bookends. Books purchased or appraised.

MURDER INK

Jay Pearsall	PHONE	1-212-362-8905
2486 Broadway	FAX	1-212-877-0112
New York NY 10025-7428 USA	TOLLFREE	1-800-488-8123
	EMAIL	info@MurderInk.com
	WEBSITE	www.murderink.com

World's first mystery bookstore. Every mystery in print plus out-of-print, rare, and signed first editions. Also mainstream fiction, children's and young adult titles. Quarterly catalog. Monthly newsletter (for buyers only). Gus the mystery hound.

MURDER, MYSTERY & MAYHEM

Yvonne & Robert Peaslee, Owners	TOLLFREE	1-866-231-7691
873 Langley Ct	EMAIL	store@mysterymayhem.com
Rochester Hills MI 48309 USA	WEBSITE	www.mysterymayhem.com

Online & mail-order only. New & "pre-read" books including children's books. Newsletter. IMBA.

MURDER ON THE BEACH MYSTERY BOOKSTORE

Joanne Sinchuk, Bookseller	PHONE	1-561-279-7790
273 Pineapple Grove Way	FAX	1-561-279-7759
Delray Beach FL 33444-3705 USA	TOLLFREE	1-877-956-7770
	EMAIL	murdermb@gate.net
	WEBSITE	www.murderonthebeach.com

Formerly **Murder on Miami Beach**. New, used, antiquarian mystery, romantic suspense, true crime & children's. Audio. Games & puzzles. Reading group. Monthly newsletter/catalog. Murder mystery entertainment. Online sales at ABE. IMBA.

MURDER ONE

Maxim Jakubowski	PHONE	+44 207 734 3483
71-73 Charing Cross Road	FAX	+44 207 734 3429
London WC2H OAA ENGLAND	EMAIL	murderone.mail@virgin.net
	WEBSITE	www.murderone.co.uk

Largest mystery bookstore in the world! Stocks all US & British titles in print. Primarily new with used, firsts & rare. Signings. Catalog of new releases.

MY BOOK HOUSE

Linda Criswell	PHONE	1-714-771-2578
3320 E Chapman Ave #307	FAX	1-714-771-9073
Orange CA 92869-3853 USA	EMAIL	criswell@earthlink.net
	WEBSITE	home.earthlink.net/~criswell/

Mail/email order only. Used/collectible/rare/first editions/signededitions of mystery & detective fiction, science fiction, modern firsts and proofs. Website features verified author signature samples.

MYSTERIES AND MORE

Janette Johnson, Owner	PHONE	1-214-823-4300
Jennifer Allen, Manager	EMAIL	mail@mysteriesandmorebooks.com
2011 Abrams Pkwy	WEBSITE	www.mysteriesandmorebooks.com
Dallas TX 75214 USA		

Used mysteries, thrillers, biographies, and history books. Paperbacks are always half price, everyday. Separate children's section with books from pre-school all the way up to Young Adult.

MYSTERIES IN THE MOUNTAINS

Mary Southworth
1314 Tunnel Rd #103
Asheville NC 28805-1667 USA

PHONE 1-828-298-0781
EMAIL mystinmts@earthlink.net
WEBSITE www.amazon.com/shops/ mystinmts
WEBSITE www.auntb3285.mybravenet.com/ contact.html

🦅+ ✉ ∅ Mail order and online. Primarily used & reader's copies, some new. Mystery, literary, Southern, SF & historical fiction.

MYSTERIES PLUS

John & Nola Hight
91711 Smith Lake Rd
Warrenton OR 97146-7209 USA

PHONE 1-503-861-0585
EMAIL mystplus@pacifier.com
WEBSITE www.abebooks.com/home/ mystplus/

🦅 ✉ ∅ Mail order mysteries, mostly hardback with some collectible paperbacks. Also non-fiction and children's titles. Online at ABE and Amazon; open by appointment only.

MYSTERIES TO DIE FOR

2940 E Thousand Oaks Blvd
Thousand Oaks CA 91362-3278
    USA

PHONE 1-805-374-0084
FAX 1-805-492-7850
EMAIL mail@mysteriestodiefor.com
EMAIL mysteries2die4@aol.com
WEBSITE www.mysteriestodiefor.com

🦅 🏛 ✉ New books, firsts, collectible. Reading group, frequent author signings. Bimonthly newsletter. Phone, mail and email orders welcome. IMBA.

THE MYSTERIOUS BOOKSHOP

Otto Penzler, Owner
129 W 56th St
New York NY 10019-3881 USA

PHONE 1-212-765-0900
FAX 1-212-265-5478
TOLLFREE 1-800-352-2840
EMAIL mysteriousny@worldnet.att.net
WEBSITE www.mysteriousbookshop.com

🦅 🏛 ✉ Mystery, crime, suspense, espionage, & detective fiction. New, firsts, rare & collectible. Monthly newsletters by mail or by email. Six collectors clubs for different interests. Signings. Free book search service. IMBA.

MYSTERIOUS GALAXY

Maryelizabeth Hart
7051 Clairemont Mesa Blvd Ste 302
San Diego CA 92111-1040 USA

PHONE 1-858-268-4747
FAX 1-858-268-4775
TOLLFREE 1-800-811-4747
EMAIL mgbooks@mystgalaxy.com
WEBSITE www.mystgalaxy.com

🦅+ 🏛 Books of Martians, Murder, Magic & Mayhem. Reading group, signings, online catalog. Newsletter. ABA, IMBA.

MYSTERIOUS SEARCH

George Parkman
PO Box 5395
Gainesville GA 30504 USA

PHONE 1-770-536-4254
FAX 1-770-536-3149
TOLLFREE 1-800-322-3620
EMAIL search@MysteriousSearch.com
WEBSITE www.MysteriousSearch.com

◖ ✉ Dedicated search service for out-of-print and hard-to-find mystery books. Accepts want lists of any length, by phone, fax, mail, or email. Contacts customer with details of found books, then handles all details of purchase and delivery.

THE MYSTERY ANNEX

1407 Ocean Front Walk
Venice CA 90291-3605 USA

PHONE 1-310-399-2360
FAX 1-310-399-4512
EMAIL info@smallworldbooks.com
WEBSITE www.smallworldbooks.com

🦅 🏚 Annex of Small World Books. Complete mystery selection and a "vampire literature" section. Primarily new, mystery & related genre. Mystery of the Month club. Signings. ABA.

MYSTERY BOOK CENTER

Leonard Bromberg
4 Jones Ave
Rumford ME 04276 USA

PHONE 1-207-364-8914
EMAIL broms1@earthlink.net
WEBSITE www.abebooks.com/home/
mysterybookcenter/

◖ ∅ First edition mystery books in hardcover and paperback from 1986 on, including new releases and ARCs. Online sales only, through ABE.

☛ THE MYSTERY BOOKSHOP (SIDNEY, BC)

Beacon Books
2372 Beacon Avenue
Sidney BC V8L 1X3 CANADA

PHONE 1-250-655-4447
FAX 1-250-655-5283
EMAIL beaconbks@pinc.com
WEBSITE www.abebooks.com/home/
beaconbks/

🦅 🏚 ∅ At the back of Beacon Books. Hardcover and paperback, anthologies, true crime. Games & puzzles. Formerly Wimsey Books in Saanichton. Online sales through ABE.

THE MYSTERY BOOKSTORE (BARRYVILLE NY)

Adrienne Williams, President
111 Route 97
PO Box 248
Barryville NY 12719-0248 USA

◖ 🏚 ✉ Open store. Mystery, detective, Sherlockian. Used, rare, firsts, out-of-print. Catalog & mail-order available. Also carries general stock. "Priority: building collections, educating clients."

THE MYSTERY BOOKSTORE (LOS ANGELES CA)

Sheldon McArthur, Managing Partner	PHONE	1-310-209-0415
Richard Brewer, Asst Mgr	FAX	1-310-209-0436
1036 Broxton Ave	TOLLFREE	1-800-821-9017
Los Angeles CA 90024-2824 USA	EMAIL	orders@mystery-bookstore.com
	WEBSITE	www.mystery-bookstore.com

🦅 📖 ∅ Full service new, used, rare, and collectible mysteries plus pre-1960 paperbacks. Events, newsletter.

THE MYSTERY BOOKSTORE (OMAHA NE)

Kate Birkel, Owner	PHONE	1-402-342-7343
1422 S 13th St	TOLLFREE	1-888-412-7343
Omaha NE 68108-3504 USA	EMAIL	kate@mysterybookstore.ws
	WEBSITE	www.mysterybookstore.ws

🦅 📖 ✉ All US books discounted. British imports. Frequent author events, reading groups. Free sample newsletter on request. Reasonable mailing rates. IMBA. Bookstore cats Sam & Ella.

THE MYSTERY COMPANY

Jim Huang, Owner	PHONE	1-317-705-9711
1323 S Rangeline Rd	FAX	1-317-705-1402
Carmel IN 46032 USA	TOLLFREE	1-800-643-6737
	EMAIL	staff@themysterycompany.com
	WEBSITE	www.themysterycompany.com

🦅 📖 ♿ New name and location for the former Deadly Passions bookstore. Mystery, SF/fantasy, romance. New and used books (mostly readers copies), some collectible. Newsletter. Want lists welcome. ABA, IMBA.

MYSTERY GUILD®

editorial:	PHONE	1-212-782-7214
1540 Broadway 16th Floor	FAX	1-212-782-7210
New York NY 10036-4094 USA	WEBSITE	www.mysteryguild.com

subscription:
6550 E 30th St
PO Box 6338
Indianapolis IN 46209-9461 USA

🦅 ✉ ∅ Members-only book club features modestly-priced hardback reprints. Mysteries by mail since 1948, now with secure online ordering.

Mystery & Imagination Bookshop/ Bookfellows Fine and Rare Books

Malcolm & Christine Bell, Proprietors
238 N Brand Blvd
Glendale CA 91203-2610 USA

PHONE 1-818-545-0079
FAX 1-818-545-0094
EMAIL bookfellows@gowebway.com
WEBSITE www.abebooks.com/home/bookfellows/

Fine used books for readers and collectors. Literature, mysteries, spy fiction, SF, horror. Bookfellows shop open daily; also mail & online ordering. Mystery & Imagination catalogs available.

Mystery Ink Bookshop

John Pitts & Thu Trang
121 Camino de la Placita
Taos NM 87571-5940 USA

PHONE 1-505-751-1092
EMAIL mystery@newmex.com
WEBSITE www.abebooks.com/home/mystery/

General used books with a specialty in mystery. Buy, sell & trade. Shop is in a beautiful old adobe building just off Taos plaza. Occasional signings.

The Mystery Lady

Catherine Hoffner
3 Castle Rd
Vincentown NJ 08088-9525 USA

PHONE 1-609-268-5754
EMAIL mysteryk@jersey.net

Mail, email, phone orders. New, slightly used, & collectible mysteries, most signed. Free searches for any type of book. Want lists welcome.

Mystery Lovers Bookshop

Mary Alice Gorman & Richard
   Goldman
514 Allegheny River Blvd
Oakmont PA 15139-1617 USA

PHONE 1-412-828-4877
FAX 1-412-828-6470
TOLLFREE 1-888-800-6078
EMAIL mysterylovers@mysterylovers.com
WEBSITE www.mysterylovers.com

Primarily new & firsts. Newsletter, gifts, many readers clubs. Espresso Bar. Children's programs. Annual **Festival of Mystery** on the Monday after Malice Domestic. Quarterly newsletter. ABA, IMBA.

Mystery Loves Company

Kathy Harig
1730 Fleet St
Baltimore MD 21231-2919 USA

PHONE 1-410-276-6708
TOLLFREE 1-800-538-0042
EMAIL kathy@mysterylovescompany.com
WEBSITE www.mysterylovescompany.com

Full service store and online ordering. Monthly email newsletter. New, used, antiquarian, some pulps, collectible paperbacks, British imports, and signed first editions. Gifts and custom gift baskets. Author signings. IMBA, SinC. Cats Nick and Nora.

MYSTERY MIKE'S

Mike Bursaw	PHONE	1-317-575-9975
101 E Carmel Dr Ste 111	FAX	1-317-575-9984
PO Box 3172	EMAIL	mbursaw@mysterymikes.com
Carmel IN 46082-3172 USA	WEBSITE	www.abebooks.com/home/ mysterymikes/

🦅 ✉ ⊘ New, used, firsts, out-of-print, and rare mystery and detective fiction. Mail order or by appointment.

THE MYSTERY NOOK

mailing:

PO Box 9411	PHONE	1-309-685-3840
Peoria IL 61612-9411 USA	EMAIL	mystnook@ocslink.com
	WEBSITE	www.ocslink.com/~mystnook/

store:

Illinois Antique Center
311 SW Water, 1st floor
Peoria IL 61603 USA

◗ 🏛 ✉ Mystery & detective fiction. Used, collectible, out-of-print; firsts & reading copies, signed, vintage. Children's mysteries. Catalog available.

MYSTERY ONE BOOKSHOP

Richard Katz	PHONE	1-414-347-4077
2109 N Prospect Ave	EMAIL	mystery1@execpc.com
Milwaukee WI 53202-1110 USA	WEBSITE	www.mysteryone.com

🦅 🏛 ✉ Mystery, spy, & suspense. New, used, and collectible books, will ship, want lists welcome. Frequent author signings. IMBA.

MYSTERY PIER BOOKS

Louis M Jason & Harvey Jason	PHONE	1-310-657-5557
8826 W Sunset Blvd	FAX	1-310-657-5566
West Hollywood CA 90069-2105	TOLLFREE	1-888-410-5557
USA	EMAIL	mysterypierbooks@aol.com
	WEBSITE	www.abebooks.com/home/ mysterypierbooks/

◗ 🏛 ⊘ Fine & rare first editions, mystery, true crime, cinema rareties, literary highspots. Collectible, signed and inscribed. ABA, ABAA, ILAB.

NEWBURN MYSTERY ETC

Maurice Newburn	PHONE	1-510-893-1370
2134 Broadway	EMAIL	newburn@newburnmystery.com
Oakland CA 94612-2310 USA	WEBSITE	www.newburnmystery.com

☼ 🏛 Formerly **M C Newburn Books**. New & used paperbacks, latest new hardbacks. Mystery reading group, many author signings. Excellent selection of local authors. Tricky the bookstore cat.

Nicholas J Certo

PO Box 10305
Newburgh NY 12552-0305 USA

PHONE 1-845-566-4188
EMAIL ncerto@frontiernet.net
WEBSITE www.abebooks.com/home/certobooks/

Mystery/detective, pulp magazines, vintage paperbacks. Firsts, collectible & rare, ephemera. Also s/f, supernatural, early illustrated books. Catalog available. Want lists welcome.

Nigel Williams Rare Books

22 & 25 Cecil Court
Charing Cross Road
London WC2N 4HE England

PHONE +44 20 7836 7757
FAX +44 20 7379 5918
EMAIL queries@nigelwilliams.com
WEBSITE www.nigelwilliams.com

Fine and rare books, modern firsts. Crime and detective fiction, Wodehouse, children's and illustrated books. "One of the finest in the UK." Regular catalogs; want lists welcome. Email newsletter. Secure online ordering. ABA(UK), ILAB.

No Alibis

David Torrrans
83 Botanic Ave
Belfast BT7 1JL Northern Ireland

PHONE +44 28 9031 9607
EMAIL david@noalibis.com
WEBSITE www.noalibis.com

Crime fiction, American studies, true life or fictional crime stories, thrillers, whodunits, mysteries, police and detective stories. Signed editions and special bookshop events including visiting authors.

Norris Books

Chuck Chavdarian, Owner
PMB 201
2491 San Ramon Valley Blvd Ste 1
San Ramon CA 94583-1677 USA

PHONE/FAX 1-925-867-1218
EMAIL norrisbooks@earthlink.net
WEBSITE www.norrisbooks.com

Primarily first edition mysteries/detective fiction & suspense; also horror, SF, fantasy, general stock. Used, firsts, collectible. Mail order. Online catalogs at ABE and Amazon.

Now Voyager Bookstore

Diane Johnson & Nan Cinnater
357 Commercial St
PO Box 551
Provincetown MA 02657-0551 USA

PHONE 1-508-487-0848
EMAIL nowvoy@capecod.net
WEBSITE www.nowvoyagerbooks.com

Seaside bookshop with "Cape and Dagger" mystery corner. Mostly new books, some used, rarely rare. Featuring Cape Cod mysteries, gay & lesbian mysteries, women detectives. Exclusive Edward Gorey T-shirts. Mail order via Website.

OLD ALGONQUIN BOOKS

John Dunning, Owner   PHONE   1-303-431-7072
PO Box 18514   EMAIL   algonquin@uswest.net
Denver CO 80218-0514 USA   WEBSITE   www.oldalgonquin.com

First edition mysteries, literature, science fiction; also history and Americana. Orders by phone or online only. ABAA, ILAB, RMABA.

THE OLD LONDON BOOKSHOP

Michael P Schon & Marlys Glaser-   PHONE   1-360-733-7273
Schon   EMAIL   OldLondon@aol.com
111 Central Ave
PO Box 922
Bellingham WA 98227-0922 USA

Mail order or by appointment. 20,000 modern first editions, 7,000 mystery hardback first editions. Also SF & fantasy, related nonfiction. Primarily for collectors. IMBA, ABAA. Cat named Hansel.

OLD PUEBLO BOOKS

Mike Walsh   PHONE   1-520-760-2745
PO Box 17898   FAX   1-800-556-9737
Tucson AZ 85731-7898 USA   EMAIL   itsmstry@aol.com
     WEBSITE   www.itsmstry.com

Signed first editions. Mystery, detective, vintage paperbacks. Search service. Online sales through ABE.

ONCE UPON A CRIME

Gary Shulze & Pat Frovarp   PHONE   1-612-870-3785
604 W 26th St   FAX   1-612-871-8880
Minneapolis MN 55405-3303 USA   EMAIL   onceuponacrime@earthlink.net

Full service mystery specialist. New, used, firsts, rare, signings. "Happy to do mail order." New owners. IMBA.

P.I. BOOKSTORE

     EMAIL   service@pibookstore.com
     WEBSITE   www.pibookstore.com

Non-fiction only. Online bookstore with reference and how-to books for the private investigator. Missing persons, criminal investigation, forensics, and surveillance. Videos and DVDs.

P.I.E.S.

Gary Warren Niebuhr   EMAIL   piesbook@execpc.com
PO Box 341218   WEBSITE   my.execpc.com/~piesbook/
Milwaukee WI 53234-1218 USA   piescatalog.html

Private Investigator Entertainment Service. New, used, collectible, rare private eye fiction by mail-order or email. Catalog available in print or online, want lists welcome. MWA, PWA.

PAGE ONE TOO ANTIQUARIAN BOOKS

Betty Parker
11200 Montgomery Blvd NE
Albuquerque NM 87111-2679 USA

PHONE 1-505-294-5623
TOLLFREE 1-800-521-4122
EMAIL david@page1book.com
WEBSITE www.page1book.com

This branch of New Mexico's largest independent bookstore specializes in used, collectible, and rare books, with extensive mystery selection. Want lists welcome; will do book searches.

PAGES FOR ALL AGES BOOKSTORE

Jonathan Graham
1201 Savoy Plaza
Savoy IL 61874-9456 USA

PHONE 1-217-351-PAGE
TOLLFREE 1-888-724-3716
WEBSITE www.pagesforallages.com
EMAIL pagesforallages@hotmail.com

Illinois' largest independent bookstore. Large mystery & suspense stock. Mystery reading group. Signings. ABA.

PANDORA'S BOOKS LTD.

Tim Friesen
PO Box 54
Neche ND 58265-0054 USA

PHONE 1-204-324-8548
FAX 1-204-324-1628
EMAIL pandora@mts.net
WEBSITE www.pandora.ca

Est. 1973. About 200,000 books. Mystery, SF, westerns, other genres. Used, firsts & rare. Online sales at ABE, Alibris, ChooseBooks, & Amazon. In-store shopping by appointment only. Catalogs available online.

PARTNERS & CRIME MYSTERY BOOKSELLERS

44 Greenwich Ave
New York NY 10011-8347 USA

PHONE 1-212-243-0440
FAX 1-212-243-4624
EMAIL partners@crimepays.com
WEBSITE www.crimepays.com

First editions and British imports. Catalog, collector recommendations. Original mystery book cover art. Meeting room, lending library, author signings. Key contacts: Days: Steve Viola, Evenings: Kate Nesbit. Store Bird in Residence: Parker.

PATTERSON SMITH

PO Box 8098
Glen Ridge NJ 07028-8098 USA

PHONE 1-973-744-3291
FAX 1-973-744-4501
EMAIL books@patterson-smith.com
WEBSITE www.patterson-smith.com

Non-fiction only. Rare & out-of-print criminal, police & prison history, trials, forensics, criminal & detective biographies, capital punishment, con games, mug shots, & wanted fliers. Catalog available, want lists welcome. ABAA, ILAB.

☛ PAULETTE GREENE RARE BOOKS

7152 Via Palomar	PHONE	1-561-347-1948
Boca Raton FL 33433 USA	EMAIL	greenebooks@juno.com
	WEBSITE	dogbert.abebooks.com/abe/Client Home?clientId=815925

Modern firsts, mystery and detective, Sherlock Holmes.

PETER L STERN & CO, INC.

55 Temple Pl	PHONE	1-617-542-2376
Boston MA 02111-1300 USA	FAX	1-617-542-3263
	EMAIL	psbook@aol.com
	WEBSITE	www.abebooks.com/home/plsabe/

Store with rare & first editions for the collector. Sherlockiana, autographed letters & MSS. Catalog available. ABAA.

PETTY BOOKS

Lorraine Petty, Prop.	PHONE	1-401-596-4932
PO Box 266	EMAIL	pettycrime@juno.com
Westerly RI 02891-0266 USA		

New, used, & collectible. All types, with special focus on post-1975 women writers. By appointment only. NEBA.

POE'S COUSIN

Anne Poe Lehr & Jonathan M Lehr	PHONE	1-914-948-0735
9 Windward Ave	FAX	1-914-946-4219
White Plains NY 10605-5306 USA	EMAIL	orders@poescousin.com
	WEBSITE	www.poescousin.com

Mysteries & detective fiction. Firsts & rare, UK & US, historical & bibliomysteries specialties. Mail order, online, & by appointment. Catalog available. Want lists welcome. ABA, IMBA, IOBA. Bookstore dog: Mad Max the basset.

THE POISONED PEN

Barbara Peters, Owner	PHONE	1-480-947-2974
4014 N Goldwater Blvd Ste 101	FAX	1-480-945-1023
Scottsdale AZ 85251-4335 USA	TOLLFREE	1-888-560-9919
	EMAIL	sales@poisonedpen.com
	WEBSITE	www.poisonedpen.com

Specializing in British & Canadian imports, historical, & Southwestern mysteries. Reading group, signings, online sales. Monthly 48-page subscription newsletter *Booknews*, email news bulletins. ABA, IMBA, Book Sense.

POLAR & CO

257 chaussee d'Ixelles	PHONE	+32 2 648 0194
1050 Brussels BELGIUM		

Small shop containing both new and used French-language mysteries and a few shelves of science fiction. Also a small section of used English-language mysteries with a sprinkling of science fiction.

POST MORTEM BOOKS

Ralph Spurrier	PHONE	+44 1273 843066
58 Stanford Ave	FAX	+44 870 161 7332
Hassocks, Sussex BN6 8JH ENGLAND	EMAIL	ralph@pmbooks.demon.co.uk
	WEBSITE	www.postmortembooks.com

Est. 1979, the oldest mystery fiction business in the UK. Catalog of new & used books that is also a newsletter, now available online. Mail-order/by appointment only. Resident cat: Reg.

PRAIRIE LIGHTS BOOKSTORE

Paul Ingram, Manager	PHONE	1-319-337-2681
15 S Dubuque St	FAX	1-319-337-2056
Iowa City IA 52240-3902 USA	TOLLFREE	1-800-295-BOOK
	EMAIL	info@prairielights.com
	WEBSITE	prairielights.com

Large, successful independent bookstore that hosts a regular author reading series. ABA, Book Sense.

PRIME CRIME BOOKS

Linda Wiken	PHONE	1-613-238-CLUE
891 Bank St	FAX	1-613-521-4808
Ottawa ON K1S 3W4 CANADA	EMAIL	prime.crime@rogers.com
	WEBSITE	www.primecrimebooks.com

New with some used paperbacks. Gifts & signings. Newsletter *Dead Write*. IMBA. Sam the bookstore skeleton.

PULP FICTION

Ron Serdiuk	PHONE	+61 7 3236 2750
shop:	FAX	+61 7 3236 2752
Shops 28-29, Anzac Square Arcade	EMAIL	pulpfiction@compuserve.com
265-269 Edward Street		
Brisbane QLD 4000 AUSTRALIA		
mailing:		
GPO Box 297		
Brisbane QLD 4001 AUSTRALIA		

SF, fantasy, crime, & mystery. Mail order, monthly catalog. New books only as of press time; plans to add used books soon.

QUAIL RIDGE BOOKS & MUSIC

Nancy Olson	PHONE	1-919-828-1588
3522 Wade Ave	FAX	1-919-828-1768
Raleigh NC 27607 USA	TOLLFREE	1-800-672-6789
	EMAIL	qrbooks1@aol.com
	WEBSITE	quailridgebooks.booksense.com

Leading regional independent bookstore. PW Bookseller of the Year 2001. Signings, discussion groups. ABA, Book Sense.

QUILL & BRUSH

Allen & Patricia Ahearn	PHONE	1-301-874-3200
1137 Sugarloaf Mountain Rd	FAX	1-301-874-0824
Dickerson MD 20842-8754 USA	EMAIL	firsts@qbbooks.com
	WEBSITE	www.qbbooks.com

⟨ ✉ First editions, signed & limited. Mysteries and literature. Bibliographies & price guides for individual authors. Books & computer programs for collectors. Open by appointment. Over 10,000 books for sale, cataloged on website. Print catalogs available. Want lists welcome. ABAA, ILAB, IOBA.

RAC BOOKS

Anne Muren & Robin Smith	PHONE	1-717-428-3776
3294 Seitzville Rd	EMAIL	books@racbooks.com
Seven Valleys PA 17360 USA	WEBSITE	www.racbooks.com
	WEBSITE	www.abebooks.com/home/racbooks/

⟨ 🏠 ∅ General stock used books, with emphasis on mysteries. Several shops in antiques centers. Frequently exhibit at book fairs.

🖝 RALPH SIPPER/ BOOKS

10 W. Micheltorena	PHONE	1-805-962-2141
Santa Barbara CA 93101 USA	FAX	1-805-966-5057
	EMAIL	carolsipper@cox.net

⟨ ✉ Mail order or by appointment only. Modern literature: First editions, manuscripts, letters, association copies. Mystery and detective fiction, cinema books, twentieth century. ABAA.

RANDOM SAMPLE

Brenda Stewart, Owner	PHONE	1-252-746-4714
4250A Lee St	FAX	1-252-746-9645
PO Box 96	EMAIL	randomsample@talkingphonebook.net
Ayden NC 28513-0096 USA		

🕊+ 🏠 Store with new and used mysteries, romance, some s.f., western. Happy to do author events. Bookstore dog: Shadow. IMBA.

THE RAVEN BOOKSTORE

Pat Kehde & Mary Lou Wright	PHONE	1-785-749-3300
6 E 7th St	FAX	1-785-843-5909
Lawrence KS 66044-2702 USA	TOLLFREE	1-888-712-7339
	EMAIL	pkraven@webserf.net
	WEBSITE	www.ravenbookstore.com

☼ 🏠 ♿ New & used. UK imports. Mystery reading groups, signings, & newsletter. Kansas State Women-Owned Business of the Year 2002. IMBA, ABA.

READ IT AGAIN, SAM

David Taylor & Eugene Ford	PHONE/FAX	1-434-977-9844
214 E Main St	EMAIL	readit@cstone.net
Charlottesville VA 22902-5232 USA	WEBSITE	www.abebooks.com/home/ readitagainsam/

Used bookstore specializing in mysteries and vintage paperbacks. Located on the downtown mall. Open daily.

READING MATTERS

Allan & Lee Walker	PHONE	+61 3 9417 7393
74 Smith St	FAX	+61 3 9417 3628
Collingwood VIC 3066 AUSTRALIA	EMAIL	bookquest@readingmatters.com.au
	WEBSITE	www.readingmatters.com.au

Mystery, detective, espionage and true crime. Modern firsts, rare & collectible. Hardcovers & pulps. Secure on-line ordering & mail order catalogs. Shop open Wed-Sat. Appointment may be required to view on-line titles; please call ahead to ensure we can assist you.

REGULATOR BOOKSHOP

Tom Campbell	PHONE	1-919-286-2700
720 9th St	FAX	1-919-286-6063
Durham NC 27705-4877 USA	EMAIL	mail@regbook.com
	WEBSITE	www.regbook.com

Small but well-known independent bookstore, good mystery section. Newsletter & reading group. Author events. Café. ABA, Book Sense.

REMEMBER THE ALIBI MYSTERY BOOKSTORE

Patsy Asher, Owner	PHONE	1-210-829-1356
8055 West Ave Ste 101	FAX	1-210-829-1250
San Antonio TX 78213-1842 USA	TOLLFREE	1-888-272-5135
	EMAIL	patsy@world-net.net
	WEBSITE	www.rememberthealibi.com

Full service mystery bookstore with games, puzzles, and books from new to rare. Signings. Mail orders welcome. Newsletter *Caught Dead in Texas*. Est. 1996. IMBA.

RICHARD WILLIAMS, BOOKDEALER

15 High St, Dragonby	PHONE	+44 1724 840645
Scunthorpe, N. Lincs. DN15 0BE	EMAIL	rah.williams@virgin.net
ENGLAND	WEBSITE	freespace.virgin.net/rah.williams

Mail order only, catalog available. All genres of popular fiction—hardcover, paperback, and periodicals, related nonfiction and miscellany. Used, rare, collectible. Publishes bibliographies & checklists for various authors & imprints.

ROBERT GAVORA, FINE AND RARE BOOKS

PO Box 448	PHONE	1-541-512-9000
Talent OR 97540-0448 USA	FAX	1-541-535-1226
	EMAIL	books@robertgavora.com
	WEBSITE	www.robertgavora.com

(✉ ⊘ Mystery, SF, civil war, railroading, the West. Mail order, online, or by appointment. ABAA.

ROYAL BOOKS

Kevin Johnson, Owner	PHONE	1-410-366-7329
32 W 25th St	FAX	1-801-740-3231
Baltimore MD 21218-5002 USA	EMAIL	royalbooks@att.net
	WEBSITE	www.royalbooksonline.com
	WEBSITE	www.abebooks.com/home/ royalbooks/

(🏛 ✉ ⊘ Fine first editions, signed and unsigned. Crime fiction, modern literature, books on film & music. Bimonthly email and printed catalog of new acquisitions. Want lists welcome. ABAA, ILAB.

THE RUE MORGUE

Tom & Enid Schantz	PHONE	1-303-443-5757
PO Box 4119	FAX	1-303-443-4010
Boulder CO 80306-4119 USA	EMAIL	Tomenid@attbi.com

(✉ Oldest mystery bookseller in business continues by mail-order, specializing in vintage used and collectible mysteries. Sells new mysteries (other than Rue Morgue Press) only at conventions. IMBA.

RUPERT BOOKS

R Dixon & Paulina M Smith	PHONE	+44 1954 781861
58/59 Stonefield	EMAIL	sales@rupert-books.co.uk
Bar Hill	WEBSITE	www.rupert-books.co.uk
Cambridge CB3 8TE ENGLAND		

§ ✉ Specialists in Sherlockiana, Doyleana, and Jack the Ripper. Mostly rare & collectible, some new. Mail-order & by appointment only. Quarterly catalogs.

SAM WELLER'S BOOKS

Tony Weller, President	PHONE	1-801-328-2586
254 S Main St	FAX	1-801-595-0051
Salt Lake City UT 84101-2077 USA	TOLLFREE	1-800-333-SAMW
	EMAIL	books@samwellers.com
	WEBSITE	www.samwellers.com

☼ 🏛 ⊘ Three floors with thousands of new, used, & rare books. Supplying Utah readers and bibliophiles everywhere since 1929. Secure online ordering. Author events. ABA, ABAA.

The San Francisco Mystery Bookstore

Diane Kudisch, Owner	PHONE	1-415-282-7444
4175 24th St	EMAIL	diane@sfmysterybooks.com
San Francisco CA 94114-3614 USA	WEBSITE	www.sfmysterybooks.com

Mysteries and books about mysteries since 1975. New & used, rare & collectible, Sherlockiana, reference, signed books. Author signing schedule available by e-mail. Want lists welcome. "Every book guaranteed to have a corpse." IMBA.

Scene of the Crime

Don & Jen Longmuir	PHONE	1-905-646-0214
PO Box 1481	FAX	1-905-562-7960
Niagara Falls NY 14302-1481 USA	EMAIL	jbartkiw@cogeco.ca
20 Hawthorne Ave	WEBSITE	www.abebooks.com/home/crime
St Catharines ON L2M 6A9 CANADA		

First edition mysteries and paperbacks; bibliomysteries, Canadian writers, sports mysteries.

Schoenhof's Foreign Books

76A Mount Auburn St	PHONE	1-617-547-8855
Cambridge MA 02138-5051 USA	FAX	1-617-547-8551
	EMAIL	info@schoenhofs.com
	WEBSITE	www.schoenhofs.com

A terrific source for original editions of non-English-language books (over 500 mystery titles in French alone). New arrivals booklist issued quarterly, available online or by mail. Est. 1856. NEBA.

Science Fiction and Mystery Bookshop, Ltd.

Mark Stevens	PHONE	1-404-634-3226
2000F Cheshire Bridge Rd NE	FAX	1-404-634-6697
Atlanta GA 30324-4273 USA	EMAIL	sfamark@aol.com
	EMAIL	sf.mystery.books@mindspring.com

Strong in true crime & hardboiled. Reading groups. Collectible, firsts, rare, as well as new.

Scotland Yard Books

Judy Duhl	PHONE	1-847-446-2214
556 Green Bay Rd	FAX	1-847-446-2210
Winnetka IL 60093-2221 USA	EMAIL	jduhl@avenew.com
	WEBSITE	scotlandyardbooks.com

New hardcovers & softcovers, used paperbacks. Author signings & "Mystery of the Month Christmas Plan." IMBA.

SEATTLE MYSTERY BOOKSHOP

J B Dickey, Proprietor	PHONE	1-206-587-5737
117 Cherry St	EMAIL	staff@seattlemystery.com
Seattle WA 98104-2205 USA	WEBSITE	www.seattlemystery.com

🐦 🏛 ✉ New, used, firsts, rare. Whodunits, detectives, suspense, thrillers, spies, and true crime. Signings. Mail order and want lists welcome. IMBA, ABA.

SECOND STORY BOOKS

Nelson Freck, Mystery & SF Dept	PHONE	1-301-468-9689 x19
12160 Parklawn Dr	FAX	1-301-770-9544
Rockville MD 20852-1708 USA	EMAIL	ssbmystery@aol.com
	WEBSITE	www.abebooks.com/home/ secondstorybooks/

🌙 🏛 ∅ Collectors showroom (open Mon–Sat 10–6) has large selection. Monthly catalog includes SF and mystery. More than 18,000 used mystery paperbacks in the main store. ABAA.

SHERLOCK HOLMES MUSEET: ANTIKVARIATET

Egebjergvej 210	PHONE	+45 5932 9238
Strandhuse	EMAIL	sherlockiana@nielsen.mail.dk
4500 Nykøbing Sjælland DENMARK	WEBSITE	www.sherlockiana.net

🌙 🏛 ✉ Shop and mail order. Used, collectible, & rare books in Danish, Swedish, and English. Crime & detective fiction, Sherlockiana, Droodiana, SF, fantasy, Wodehouse. Online catalog. Want lists welcome. ILAB.

SHERLOCK IN L.A.

Vincent & Flavia Brosnan	PHONE	1-760-630-2013
1741 Via Allena	EMAIL	sherlockinla@cox.net
Oceanside CA 92056-6216 USA		

§ ✉ Mail order or by appointment only. Used, collectible, and rare. Specializing in Doyle, Sherlockiana, Victoriana. Occasional related art & true crime. Audio, video, ephemera.

SHERLOCK'S HOME MYSTERY BOOKSTORE & ENGLISH TEAROOM

Jane Hooper, Proprietor	EMAIL	jane@sherlockshome.com
11 E Kansas St	WEBSITE	www.sherlockshome.com
Liberty MO 64068 USA		

🐦 🏛 First editions, new, used, and out-of-print. Gifts and accessories for readers. Book clubs, signings. IMBA.

SHERLOCKIANA—LIBRERIA DEL GIALLO

Tecla Dozio	PHONE	+39 2 3453 5073
Via Peschiera 1	WEBSITE	www.alice.it/news/primo/
20154 Milano ITALY		sherlock.htm

🐦 🏛 First mystery specialty store in Italy. Excellent stock of titles in Italian. New, used, reader's. Signings. Archives of Sherlockiana.

SHERWOOD FINE BOOKS

Bill & Joan Sherwood
5911 E Spring St #402
Long Beach CA 90808-3700 USA

PHONE 1-562-421-8161
EMAIL bsherwoodbooks@cs.com

⚲ ✉ Modern literary firsts—fiction, detective, SF, horror. Mail order only. Catalogs available.

THE SILVER DOOR

Karen LaPorte, Proprietor
PO Box 3208
Redondo Beach CA 90277-1208 USA

PHONE 1-310-379-6005

⚲ ✉ Fine first editions, signed & review copies; collectibles. Visitors welcome by appointment; please telephone. Catalog available, want lists welcome, free search service. Reviews for various publications.

THE SLEUTH OF BAKER STREET

J D Singh & Marian Misters
1600 Bayview Ave
Toronto ON M4G 3B7 CANADA

PHONE 1-416-483-3111
FAX 1-416-483-3141
EMAIL sleuth@inforamp.net
WEBSITE www.abebooks.com/home/ sleuthbooks/

🦅 🏠 ♿ ✉ ⌀ Full service shop. New, used, collectible, rare and first editions. Mysteries, thrillers, spy, Sherlockiana. Also mail order; want-lists welcome. Newsletter *The Merchant of Menace*. IMBA, CBA. Cats: Paddington & Princess.

THE SLY FOX

George Fox Rishel, Proprietor
123 N Springfield St
PO Box 117
Virden IL 62690-0117 USA

PHONE 1-217-965-3641
TOLLFREE 1-877-848-3100
EMAIL slyfox@ctllc.com
WEBSITE www.abebooks.com/home/ slyfoxone/

🦅 🏠 First editions & paperbacks, some reprints; emphasis on historical mysteries, Illinois settings, British imports, Sherlock Holmes, British hard boiled and noir, Native American and Western American mysteries, out-of-print editions. New books only. Open daily. IMBA, ABA, GLBA.

SNOOP SISTERS BOOKSHOPPE & BOUTIQUE

Susan Rose, President
11 Sunset Bay Dr
Clearwater FL 33756-1644 USA

PHONE/FAX 1-727-586-2317
EMAIL srose@tampabay.rr.com

🦅+ ✉ Store closed but still selling by mail order. New books, gifts. Newsletter *The Snooper*. IMBA.

SOMETHING WICKED BOOKS & MORE

Linda DeWoskin	PHONE	1-847-328-1300
816 Church St	FAX	1-847-491-1839
Evanston IL 60201-3707 USA		

Primarily new, some used. Gifts, readers group, signings. Monthly email newsletter, bookwatch notification service, book club. IMBA.

THE SPACE-CRIME CONTINUUM

Chris Aylott & Deb Tomaselli	PHONE	1-413-584-0994
92 King St	TOLLFREE	1-888-844-8924
Northampton MA 01060-3257 USA	EMAIL	books@spacecrime.com
	WEBSITE	www.spacecrime.com

New and used science fiction, mysteries, games and historical fiction. Online catalog & sales. ABA, IMBA, NEBA. Bookstore cat: Otis.

SPENSER'S MYSTERY BOOKSHOP

Andrew Thurnauer & Kathy Phillips	PHONE	1-617-262-0880
223 Newbury St	FAX	1-978-725-8297
Boston MA 02116-2568 USA	EMAIL	spensers@spensersmysterybooks.com
	WEBSITE	www.spensersmysterybooks.com

Est. 1983. Over 10,000 mysteries, new & used, hardcover & paperback. Secure online ordering. IMBA.

STEVE LEWIS, BOOKSELLER

62 Chestnut Rd	PHONE	1-860-667-1574
Newington CT 06111-1601 USA	EMAIL	lewis@ntplx.net
	WEBSITE	www.lewis-books.com

Mail order paperbacks: mysteries, westerns, science fiction, Gothic & regency romance. Lists available on line.

STEVE'S SUNDRY BOOKS AND MAGAZINES

Julie Buckley	PHONE	1-918-743-3544
2612 S Harvard Ave	FAX	1-918-743-5912
Tulsa OK 74114-4603 USA	TOLLFREE	1-888-743-0989
	EMAIL	info@stevessundrybooksmags.com
	WEBSITE	www.stevessundrybooksmags.com

A Tulsa tradition for over 50 years with an old-fashioned soda-fountain counter. Developing a large mystery department. ABA.

STEVEN C BERNARD—FIRST EDITIONS

15011 Plainfield Ln	PHONE	1-301-948-8423
Darnestown MD 20874-3403 USA	FAX	1-301-947-8223
	EMAIL	scb.books@erols.com
	WEBSITE	www.scb-firsts.com

Modern firsts including detective/mystery, SF/fantasy/horror, black literature, and "books into film." Mail order or by appointment. Catalog available for $10 (refundable with purchase).

STRANGE BIRDS BOOKS

Ken Hughes, Owner	PHONE	1-513-631-3336
PO Box 12639	FAX	1-513-631-5053
Norwood OH 45212-0639 USA	TOLLFREE	1-888-917-3336
	EMAIL	strngbirds@aol.com
	WEBSITE	www.abebooks.com/home/ strangebirds/

⟨ ✉ ⌀ Affordable used paperback & hardcover mysteries. Reading copies and collectible. First editions, many signed, & vintage paperbacks. Mail order & by appointment. Want lists welcome. IMBA.

A TALE OF TWO SISTERS

Charlene Coffield	PHONE	1-817-329-0988
1401 Emerald Cir	EMAIL	shop@2sistersbooks.com
Southlake TX 76092-3307 USA	WEBSITE	www.2sistersbooks.com

⟨ ✉ ⌀ 20th century fiction in the first edition. Quality books purchased and sold. Occasional catalogues. Publisher of *Notable Literary Awards for Fiction*. Mail-order/email/ online/by appointment only. NTBA.

TALES FROM A RED HERRING

Peggy Pokorski, Purveyor	PHONE	1-415-922-8534
1556R Green St	FAX	1-415-922-8538
San Francisco CA 94123-5138 USA	TOLLFREE	1-800-922-8534
	EMAIL	PPokorski@aol.com

🦅 ✉ New hardcover & softcover books by mail order only.

TATORT

Christine & Klaus Gümpel	PHONE	+49 621 10049
Q 3 15	FAX	+49 621 10071
68161 Mannheim GERMANY		

🦅 🏠 Crime Scene. Primarily new, some used & reference. Signings.

TATTERED COVER BOOKSTORE

Cherry Creek:	1ST AVE	1-303-322-7727
2955 E 1st Ave	LODO	1-303-436-1070
Denver CO 80206-5626 USA	TOLLFREE	1-800-833-9327
LoDo:	EMAIL	books@tatteredcover.com
1628 16th St	WEBSITE	www.tatteredcover.com
Denver CO 80202-1308 USA		

☼ 🏠 One of the largest independent bookstores. Extensive mystery selection, mystery book club. Many events. Newsletter at website or by email.

THADDEUS BOOKS

4404 NE Going St	PHONE	1-503-281-6689
Portland OR 97218-1626 USA	EMAIL	mail@thaddeusbooks.com
	WEBSITE	www.thaddeusbooks.com

⟨ ✉ Mail order only. General selection with lots of mystery. Online catalog; order by phone, email or mail.

THOMAS BOOKS

Tom Miller	PHONE	1-623-247-9289
PO Box 14036	FAX	1-480-945-1023
Phoenix AZ 85063-4036 USA	EMAIL	sales@thomasbooks.com
	WEBSITE	www.thomasbooks.com

⟨ ✉ Specializing in first editions, mysteries, science fiction, fantasy, horror, signed & limited editions. Catalogues issued. ABA.

THOMPSON RARE BOOKS

Michael John Thompson	PHONE	1-250-384-9977
950 Fort Street	EMAIL	mjt@mjtbooks.com
Victoria BC V8V 3K2 CANADA	WEBSITE	www.mjtbooks.com

⟨ ⌂ ∅ First editions, detective and mystery fiction, SF, & F, illustrated books. Open store on Antique Row. Secure online ordering at website. ABAC, ILAB.

THRILLERBOEKWINKEL ALIBI

Inez Abell, Owner	PHONE/FAX	+31 20 625 0676
Willemsstraat 21	EMAIL	alibi@thrillerboekwinkel.nl
1015 Amsterdam NETHERLANDS	WEBSITE	crime.nl/alibi/

🦅 ⌂ ♿ Est. 1996. First mystery bookstore in the Netherlands. American, English, and Dutch mysteries and translations. Some hardcovers, mostly softcovers. New, used, rare. Bookstore dog: Charley.

TIME AND AGAIN BOOKS

Dennis & Eileen Ferado, Owners	PHONE/FAX	1-212-599-4542
320 E 46th St #34G	EMAIL	ferado@aol.com
New York NY 10017-3039 USA	WEBSITE	www.abebooks.com/home/
		tmndgnbk/

⟨ ✉ ∅ Mail order/online/by appointment only. Est. 1994. Mystery & detective fiction, modern literature, science fiction. New, used, collectible, and rare. Catalog available. Want lists welcome. ABAA.

TWENTIETH CENTURY FIRST EDITIONS

Jan O'Nale	PHONE	1-540-864-6288
RR 2 Box 1293	FAX	1-540-864-6088
New Castle VA 24127-9430 USA	EMAIL	20thcentury@cheapst.com
	WEBSITE	www.cheapst.com/twenty.html

⟨ ✉ Firsts & rare editions for collectors. Mystery, detective, adventure, suspense; SF-F, WWII, books about books, books into movies, modern lit.

UFO Buchhandlung

Robert Schekulin	PHONE	+49 761 33316
Rathausgasse 46	FAX	+49 761 24516
79098 Freiburg GERMANY	EMAIL	ufobuch@aol.com
	WEBSITE	www.ufo-freiburg.de

🦅+ 🏛 SF, fantasy, & horror, with "Krimis im UFO," a crime fiction shop within a shop. New and used books.

Uncle Buck's Mysteries

Roger Wuller	PHONE/FAX	1-618-397-3568
390 Oak Hill Dr	EMAIL	unclebuck@peaknet.net
Belleville IL 62223-2232 USA	WEBSITE	www.peaknet.net/~unclebuck/
	WEBSITE	www.abebooks.com/home/uncle_buck/

🦅 ✉ ⊘ Mail order only. New and used, rare, first editions, and reprint hardbacks. Online sales through ABE. Frequent catalogs.

Uncle Edgar's Mystery Bookstore

Jeff Hatfield, Manager	PHONE	1-612-824-9984
2864 Chicago Ave	FAX	1-612-827-6394
Minneapolis MN 55407-1320 USA	EMAIL	unclehugo@aol.com
	WEBSITE	www.UncleEdgar.com

🦅 🏛 One of the oldest and largest, est. 1980. New & used mystery, suspense & true crime, gifts & accessories. Signings. Quarterly newsletter in conjunction with sister store, Uncle Hugo's Science Fiction Bookstore.

Under-Cover Krimi & Hörbuch

Juliane Hansen	PHONE	+49 711 234 9943
Nesenbachstr. 50	FAX	+49 711 234 9946
70178 Stuttgart GERMANY	EMAIL	J.Hansen@under-cover.de
	WEBSITE	www.under-cover.de

🦅 🏛 Wide range of new books in crime and mystery fiction, as well as all kinds of audio books, in both German and English.

The Usual Suspects

Jeff Coopman	PHONE	1-905-227-4897
2 Barbican Gate	EMAIL	suspect@iaw.on.ca
Saint Catharines ON L2T 3Z7	WEBSITE	www.abebooks.com/home/
CANADA		usualsuspects/

🦅 ✉ ⊘ Mysteries, modern first editions and Canadian literature. Bibliomysteries a specialty, many signed, catalog available...soon. Accepts email, phone, online orders; open by appointment. Want lists welcome.

VAGABOND BOOKS

Craig Graham
3148 Club Dr
Los Angeles CA 90064 USA

PHONE 1-310-442-BOOK
EMAIL vagabondbk@aol.com
WEBSITE www.abebooks.com/home/
vagabondbooks/

Modern literature, detective & mystery fiction, horror, science fiction. By appointment. ABAA, ABA.

VAMP & TRAMP, BOOKSELLERS

Bill & Vicky Stewart, Owners
2805 2nd Ave S #100
Birmingham AL 35233-2811 USA

EMAIL mail@vampandtramp.com
WEBSITE www.abebooks.com/home/vtbooks/

Mystery stock is 95% first editions, both modern and antiquarian. Condition is paramount. Open shop. ABAA, ILAB.

VILLAGE BOOK & STATIONERY

Beth & Phillip Black
8702 Pacific
Omaha NE 68114 USA

PHONE 1-402-391-0100
FAX 1-402-391-1327

Hosts "Killing Time" mystery reading group.

VINTAGE BOOKS

Becky Milner, Owner
6613 E Mill Plain Blvd
Vancouver WA 98661-7457 USA

PHONE 1-360-694-9519
FAX 1-360-694-7644
TOLLFREE 1-888-694-9519
EMAIL staff@vintage-books.com
ORDERS books@vintage-books.com
WEBSITE www.Vintage-Books.com

General new, used, collectible, rare books with a large mystery section and limited true crime. Est. 1975. ABA. Bookstore cats: Henry & Eliza.

DIE WENDELTREPPE BUCHHANDLUNG

Jutta Wilkesmann, Owner
Brückenstrasse 34
60594 Frankfurt am Main GERMANY

PHONE +49 69 611341
FAX +49 69 613141

The Spiral Staircase. Germany's oldest mystery bookstore, est. 1989.

WF ANTIKVARIAT

Jan B Steffensen
Sdr Tranders Bygade 23
9260 Gistrup DENMARK

EMAIL wfanti@webfic.dk
WEBSITE www.webfic.dk/wfanti/wfanti.htm

Mail order and online sales only. Mystery specialist, new, used, and collectible books, specializing in Scandinavian editions, but has English books also. Online catalog available. Electronic submission of want lists. Website in Danish.

WHODUNIT? BOOKS (OLYMPIA WA)

301 E 4th Ave	PHONE	1-360-352-8252
Olympia WA 98501-1106 USA	FAX	1-360-352-8264
	EMAIL	whodunitsNW@aol.com

New and used mysteries, suspense, thrillers, true crime. Music to read by. Mail and special·orders welcome. Author signings. ABA, IMBA. Store mascot: Sherlock Owl (ceramic).

WHODUNIT? MYSTERY BOOKSTORE (WINNIPEG MB)

Gaylene Chesnut & Henrietta Wilde	PHONE	1-204-284-9100
165 Lilac St	FAX	1-204-453-5351
Winnipeg MB R3M 2S1 CANADA	TOLLFREE	1-800-468-4216
	EMAIL	info@whodunitcanada.com
	WEBSITE	www.whodunitcanada.com

New & used mystery books, modern British & Canadian first editions. Gifts, signings, newsletter *The Missing Clue*. IMBA, CBA.

WHODUNIT? (PHILADELPHIA PA)

Art Bourgeau & Henry Reifsnyder, Owners	PHONE	1-215-567-1478
	TOLLFREE	1-800-567-1478
1931 Chestnut St	EMAIL	books@whodunitphilly.com
Philadelphia PA 19103-3530 USA	WEBSITE	www.abebooks.com/home/whodunit/

New & used, recent & old. Mystery, suspense, espionage, horror, true crime. Over 100,000 titles in stock. Est. 1977.

WOLFSHEAD GALLERY

Joseph & Nickolas Linzalone	PHONE	1-201-727-1441
PO Box 506	EMAIL	wolfshead@erols.com
Ridgewood NJ 07451-0506 USA	WEBSITE	www.abebooks.com/home/wolfshead/

Dealing in collectible and rare mystery first editionsof American andBritish authors. Also Ancient & Medieval coins and archaeological objects. Catalogs issued. Visitors by appointment.

WOMEN & CHILDREN FIRST

Linda Bubon	PHONE	1-773-769-9299
5233 N Clark St	FAX	1-773-769-6729
Chicago IL 60640-2122 USA	EMAIL	wcfbooks@aol.com
	WEBSITE	www.womenandchildrenfirst.com

Feminist literature with growing mystery department, particularly books by women. Signings. ABA, Book Sense.

WRIGLEY-CROSS BOOKS

Paul Wrigley & Debbie Cross	PHONE	1-503-281-9449
1809 NE 39th Ave	TOLLFREE	1-877-694-1467
Portland OR 97212-5302 USA	EMAIL	wrigcros@teleport.com
	WEBSITE	www.teleport.com/~wrigcros/

☼ 🏛 New, used, collectible, signed. SF, fantasy, horror, mystery, & general stock. Catalog available, featuring many small presses, British, & Australian. IMBA.

WYSIWYG COLLECTIBLES & BOOKS

Thom Walls, Proprietor	PHONE	1-206-721-2598
PO Box 1095	EMAIL	WYSIWYGBooks@cs.com
Renton WA 98057-1095 USA	WEBSITE	dogbert.abebooks.com/abe/ ClientHome?clientId=944137

📞 ✉ ∅ Email/online/convention book dealers. Mystery, science fiction, westerns, maritime, paperback collectibles. Online catalog at ABE.

ZARDOZ BOOKS

Maurice Flanagan	PHONE	+44 1373 865371
20 Whitecroft	FAX	+44 1373 303984
Dilton Marsh	EMAIL	mflanagan@zardozbooks.co.uk
Westbury, Wiltshire BA13 4DJ	WEBSITE	www.zardozbooks.com
ENGLAND	WEBSITE	www.zardozbooks.co.uk

📞 ✉ ∅ Mail order & by appointment. Large purpose-built warehouse holding 70,000 hardbacks and paperbacks. Crime fiction & other genres, plus books on collecting paperbacks & pulps, cover-picture cards. Online sales and auctions. Print catalogs available.

Associations

221b — Deutscher Sherlock-Holmes-Club

Olaf H Maurer
PO Box 150314
67028 Ludwigshafen GERMANY
PHONE/FAX +49 621 675252
EMAIL olaf.maurer@221b-DSHC.de
§ German Sherlockian society.

813: Les Amis de la Littérature Policière

Jean-Louis Touchant
22 bd Richard-Lenoir
75011 Paris FRANCE
EMAIL bfremont@club-internet.fr
⚥ Association of over 800 French mystery writers and fans, est. 1979. Quarterly journal also called *813*. Gives trophies in several categories. *813* is the title of a novel by Maurice Leblanc, creator of Arsène Lupin.

American Crime Writers League

Joan Lowery Nixon, Membership
10215 Cedar Creek Dr
Houston TX 77042-2049 USA
WEBSITE www.acwl.org
⚥ Membership organization for published crime writers. Bimonthly newsletter, *The BULLETin*. Gives the annual **Ellen Nehr Award** for excellence in mystery reviewing.

Les Amis de Georges Simenon

Michel Schepens
Beigemsesteenweg 291
1852 Beigem (Grimbergen)
BELGIUM
PHONE/FAX +32 2 269 4787
EMAIL michel.schepens@win.be
☆ Publishes the *Cahiers Simenon*.

The Arsenic and Oolong Society

Brian Foust
2442 Galaxy Ln
Indianapolis IN 46229-1176 USA
PHONE 1-317-895-8773
EMAIL mirbane@JustCatholic.net
⚥ An international mystery fan group which meets monthly in Indianapolis. Fan guests of honor at Magna cum Murder IV.

The Arthur Conan Doyle Society

Christopher & Barbara Roden
PO Box 1360
Ashcroft BC V0K 1A0 CANADA
PHONE 1-250-453-2045
FAX 1-250-453-2075
EMAIL ashtree@ash-tree.bc.ca
WEBSITE www.ash-tree.bc.ca/acdsocy.html
☆ To bring together fans and promote the works of Arthur Conan Doyle. Publishes semiannual journal *ACD*.

Asociacion Internacional de Escritores Policiacos

⚥ See International Association of Crime Writers.

August Derleth Society

Kay Price, Exec Sec	PHONE	1-608-643-3242
PO Box 481	EMAIL	kprice@midplains.net
Sauk City WI 53583-0481 USA	WEBSITE	www.derleth.org

☆ Since 1978, promoting the work of August Derleth, creator of Solar Pons, the best of the Sherlock Holmes pastiches. Derleth also founded Arkham House Publishing, source of all H.P. Lovecraft writings, and wrote close to 200 books in many genres. Quarterly newsletter. Reprints of Derleth's work available for sale.

The Baker Street Irregulars

Michael Whelan, "Wiggins"
7938 Mill Stream Circle
Indianapolis IN 46278-2105 USA

§ The oldest Sherlockian fan organization, est. 1933, with hundreds of local societies (called scions), events & dinners. Publishes *The Baker Street Journal.*

The Baskerville Hall Club of Sweden

Anders Wiggström	PHONE	+46 8 25 09 35
Byggmästarvägen 29	EMAIL	wiggström@telia.com
168 32 Bromma SWEDEN	WEBSITE	hem.passagen.se/bvhall/

§ Sherlock Holmes society of Sweden. Est. 1979. Publishes *The Moor,* quarterly, and *STS,* annually.

Le Centre d'Études Georges Simenon

Prof Danielle Bajomée, Directeur	WEBSITE	www.ulg.ac.be/libnet/simenon.htm
Université de Liège		
Place Cockerill, 3		
B-4000 Liège BELGIUM		

☆ Est. 1976 for the development and dissemination of studies of Simenon's work. Sponsors a colloquium every two years, and an annual review, *Traces.*

Cloak and Clue Society

c/o Beth Fedyn	WEBSITE	www.execpc.com/~piesbook/
2816 N Interlaken Dr		cloak.html
Oconomowoc WI 53066-4909 USA	EMAIL	bfedyn@gdinet.com

🖅 Mystery readers and writers in the greater Milwaukee area. Meeting monthly since 1980. Newsletter *The Cloak.*

Il Club del Giallo

Giuseppe Isnardi	PHONE	+39 81 556 1029
Strada Genova 313	EMAIL	vdefalco@libero.it
10024 Moncalieri (TO) ITALY	EMAIL	giuseppe.isnardi@tiscalinet.it
	WEBSITE	www.fogliogiallo.it

🖅 Readers club. Members-only conference. Semiannual publication *Foglio Giallo.*

CRIME WRITERS ASSOCIATION OF AUSTRALIA

David Honeybone, Secretary   FAX   +61 3 9443 7943
c/o Preston Lower Post Office   EMAIL   nedkellynews@yahoo.com.au
3 Gilbert Road
Preston VIC 3072 AUSTRALIA

☞ Established 1995 to promote and publicize Australian crime fiction. Gives the annual **Ned Kelly Awards**. Email newsletter is the *Ned Kelly News*.

THE CRIME WRITERS' ASSOCIATION

Liz Evans, Secretary   WEBSITE   www.thecwa.co.uk
PO Box 273   EMAIL   smithie.evans@tesco.net
Borehamwood, Herts WD6 2XA
     ENGLAND

☞ Association of published writers of crime fiction & nonfiction. Gives **Dagger Awards** in several categories. Newsletter *Red Herrings*. Annual conference.

CRIME WRITERS OF CANADA

3007 Kingston Road, Box 113   PHONE   1-416-461-9876
Scarborough ON M1M 1P1   FAX   1-416-461-4489
     CANADA   EMAIL   info@crimewriterscanada.com
                               WEBSITE   www.crimewriterscanada.com

☞ For promotion of Canadian publications on crime, both fiction & true crime. Gives **Arthur Ellis Awards**. Quarterly newsletter, *Fingerprints*.

CRIME WRITERS OF SCANDINAVIA

Kim Småge   EMAIL   ksmaage@online.no
Post Box 2120 Sentrum
7411 Trondheim NORWAY

☞ Founded 1991. Includes five Scandinavian countries. Annual conference, **Glass Key Award**. Newsletter *Gränsfallet*. Also known as SKS. Affiliated with IACW.

CRIMEWRITERS QUEENSLAND

PO Box 200   FAX   +61 7 3397 0431
Holland Park   EMAIL   crimewritersq@powerup.com.au
Brisbane QLD 4121 AUSTRALIA   WEBSITE   cwpp.slq.qld.gov.au/crimewriters

☞ A publishing group run by Queensland authors to promote crime fiction in Australia's Sunshine State. Short-story anthologies available by mail order. Book and author info at website.

DET DANSKE KRIMINALAKADEMI

Birgit Brunsted, President   PHONE   +45 3860 4307
Håbets Allé 28
2700 Brønshøj DENMARK

☞ Danish Academy for Crime Fiction, est. 1986. Gives **Palle Rosenkrantz Award** for best Danish crime novel of the year.

DAPA-EM

Art Scott   PHONE   1-925-447-8269
855 Mayview Way   EMAIL   artscott@pacbell.net
Livermore CA 94550-5803 USA

☞ Each member writes a fanzine of reviews, checklists, profiles, articles. 6 issues per year. Name is anagram of "Elementary, My Dear APA" (Amateur Publishing Association). Membership limited to 35, waiting list.

THE DETECTION CLUB

WEBSITE   www.cs.appstate.edu/~sjg/
detectionclub.html

☞ Founded in1928 in London, England, this is a private, invitation-only, club of distinguished crime writers. Members take an oath to play fair with readers. They have published several collaborative novels, which are listed at this unofficial website.

THE DOROTHY L SAYERS SOCIETY

Christopher Dean, Chairman   PHONE   +44 1273 833444
Rose Cottage, Malthouse Lane   FAX   +44 1273 835988
Hurstpierpoint, West Sussex   EMAIL   info@sayers.org.uk
   BN6 9JY ENGLAND   WEBSITE   www.sayers.org.uk

☆ Est. 1976. Regular meetings & annual conference. Bimonthly newsletter. Archives open to members only.

DOROTHYL

Diane K Kovacs & Kara L Robin-   WEBSITE   www.dorothyl.com
   son, Moderators

⌀ The oldest and largest mystery email discussion group on the Internet, established in 1991. Instructions for subscribing are at the website.

THE EDGAR ALLAN POE SOCIETY OF BALTIMORE

Jeffrey A Savoye, Secretary-Treasurer   WEBSITE   www.eapoe.org
3301 Woodside Ave
Parkville MD 21234-4806 USA

☆ Since 1923, promoting the understanding of Poe's life and writings, and his associations with Baltimore. Annual lecture on 1st Sunday in October. Website has lecture transcripts and other articles on Poe.

THE EDGAR WALLACE SOCIETY

Miss Penny Wyrd, Facilitator   EMAIL   info@EdgarWallace.org
84 Ridgefield Rd   WEBSITE   www.EdgarWallace.org
Oxford OX4 3DA ENGLAND

☆ Founded 1969. Publishes quarterly *Crimson Circle Magazine*. Members in 20 countries. New members receive biography & bibliography.

THE ELIZABETH LININGTON SOCIETY

Rinehart Skeen Potts, Editor &   PHONE   1-856-589-1571
   Director
1223 Glen Terrace
Glassboro NJ 08028-1315 USA
   ☆ For fans of Barbara Elizabeth Linington, who also wrote as Leslie Egan, Egan
O'Neill, Ann Blaisdell, and Dell Shannon. Bimonthly newsletter, *The Linington Lineup*.
Also has a private archive.

FÖRENINGEN KRIMINALFÖRFATTARE I STOCKHOLM

Olov Svedelid
Österlånggatan 14
111 31 Stockholm SWEDEN
   ⚑ Crime Writers of Stockholm. Est. 1977.

THE FRANCO-MIDLAND HARDWARE CO.

Phillip Weller, Managing Director   EMAIL   sherlock.fmhc@btinternet.com
6 Bramham Moor   WEBSITE   www.btinternet.com/
Hill Head   ~sherlock.fmhc/
Fareham, Hampshire PO14 3RU
   ENGLAND
   § International Sherlock Holmes Study Group. Possibly the most active Sherlockian
organization in the world, with over 20 "branch offices," and members in more than 40
countries.

FRIEDRICH GLAUSER GESELLSCHAFT E.V.

Dr. Angelika Jockers   PHONE   +49 89 291 62282
Metzstrasse 19   FAX   +49 89 291 264
81667 München GERMANY   EMAIL   jockers.angelika@t-online.de
                              WEBSITE   www.friedrichglauser.de

   ☆ An association for fans and students of the work of the father of the German crime
novel.

FRIENDS OF MYSTERY

PO Box 8251   PHONE   1-503-241-0759
Portland OR 97207-8251 USA   FAX   1-503-241-5621
                                     EMAIL   info@friendsofmystery.org
                                     WEBSITE   www.friendsofmystery.org

   ⚑ Bimonthly speakers. Newsletter: *The Blood-Letter*. Gives the **Spotted Owl Award**
for best mystery by a writer from the Pacific Northwest.

GASLIGHT

Stephen Davies & Diana Patterson   EMAIL   Gaslight-Safe@MtRoyal.ca
                                     WEBSITE   gaslight.mtroyal.ca

   ⌀ Internet discussion list that reviews one story a week from the genres of mystery,
adventure and The Weird, written between 1800 and 1919. The current readings and
selected ones from the past are available at the website.

GENOOTSCHAP VAN NEDERLANDSTALIGE MISDAADAUTEURS

Charles den Tex, President	EMAIL	alwin@van-ee.nl
Alwin van Ee, Secretary	WEBSITE	www.crime.nl
Van Galenstraat 21		
2518 EN The Hague NETHERLANDS		

☞ GNM. Crime Writers Association of the Netherlands and Flanders (Dutch-speaking Belgium). Awards the **Gouden Strop** for best crime novel. Affiliated with IACW.

HARRY STEPHEN KEELER SOCIETY

Richard Polt	PHONE	1-513-591-1226
4745 Winton Rd	EMAIL	polt@xavier.xu.edu
Cincinnati OH 45232-1522 USA	WEBSITE	xavier.xu.edu/~polt/keeler.html

☆ Aficionados of a little-known mystery author "whose books feature preposterously convoluted 'webwork' plots, bizarre motifs and frenzied narration." *Keeler News* newsletter, 5 per year.

THE HISTORICAL MYSTERY APPRECIATION SOCIETY

Sue Feder	PHONE	1-410-847-9737
3 Goucher Woods Ct	FAX	1-410-847-9303
Towson MD 21286-5658 USA	WEBSITE	mywebpages.comcast.net/ monkshould/hmas-index.html
	EMAIL	monkshould@comcast.net

☞ Newsletter, *Murder:Past Tense*, is on sabbatical for 2003–2004, but on-line reading group continues. Gives the **Herodotus Awards**.

THE HISTORICAL NOVEL SOCIETY

Marilyn Sherlock, Membership	PHONE	+44 752 872112
38 The Fairway	EMAIL	histnovel@aol.com
Newton Ferrers, Devon PL8 1DP	WEBSITE	www.historicalnovelsociety.com
ENGLAND		

☞ Founded 1997 by Richard Lee. Semiannual magazine *Solander* with news, reviews, interviews & fiction. Quarterly *Historical Novels Review* of all new releases in UK & US.

☞ HOUNDS OF THE INTERNET

	WEBSITE	www.bcpl.lib.md.us/~lmoskowi/ hounds/hounds.html

§ Webpage explains how to subscribe to the electronic mailing list for Sherlockian (or Holmesian, as you prefer) devotees. Also archives the most recent week's messages.

IACW, AUSTRIA

Helga Anderle	EMAIL	wienerblut1@chello.at
Keinergasse 21/12		
1030 Wien AUSTRIA		

☞ Austrian branch of International Association of Crime Writers.

IACW, BELGIUM

Bob Mendes
Wezelsebaan, 191
2900 Schoten BELGIUM
    EMAIL   bob.mendes@planetinternet.be

➢ Belgian branch of the International Association of Crime Writers.

IACW, BULGARIA

Dr Svetoslav Slavchev
ul. A.P. Chekhov bl. 58 A
1113 Sofia BULGARIA

➢ Bulgarian branch of International Association of Crime Writers.

IACW, CHINA

Mr. Bao Feng, Director, International
   Division
Suite 2207, No. 168-172 Yu Yuan Rd.
Universal Mansions
200040 Shanghai CHINA

➢ Chineses contact for International Association of Crime Writers.

IACW, CUBA

José Latour
Apartado Postal 6067
CP 10600 Habana CUBA
    EMAIL   alaiep@cubarte.cult.cu

➢ Cuban contact for the International Association of Crime Writers.

IACW, CZECH REPUBLIC

Andrea Vernerová
PO Box 7
111 21 Praha 1 CZECH REPUBLIC
    EMAIL   ada99@mbox.vol.cz
    WEBSITE   www.mvcr.cz/detektiv/

➢ Czech branch of International Association of Crime Writers.

IACW, FRANCE

Virginie Brac
24 bis, rue de l'Abbé Grégoire
75006 Paris FRANCE
    PHONE/FAX   +33 142 22 25 29
    EMAIL   virginiebrac@free.fr

➢ French branch of the International Association of Crime Writers.

IACW, GERMANY

Thomas Przybilka
Buschstrasse 14
53113 Bonn GERMANY
    PHONE   +49 228 24 21 383
    FAX   +49 228 24 21 385
    EMAIL   mlbonn@t-online.de

➢ German branch of the International Association of Crime Writers.

☛ IACW, Italy

Gianfranco Orsi — EMAIL — gforsi@yahoo.it
Via Saldini 4
20100 Milano ITALY
  ✍ Italian branch of the International Association of Crime Writers.

IACW, Mexico

Paco Ignacio Taibo II — EMAIL — marinataibo3@aol.com
Atlixco 163A — EMAIL — marianataibo3@yahoo.com.mx
Colonia Condesa DF 06140
  MEXICO
  ✍ Mexican branch of the International Association of Crime Writers.

IACW, Spain

Fernando Martínez Laínez — PHONE — +34 91 351 5064
Calle Gómez Tejedor 20 — EMAIL — fml@eresmas.net
La Cerca 2
28024 Pozuelo de Alarcón, Madrid
  SPAIN
  ✍ Spanish branch of the International Association of Crime Writers.

IACW, United Kingdom

Janet Laurence — EMAIL — janetlaurence@compuserve.com
Conifers
Mayfield Close
Galhampton
Yeovil, Somerset BA22 7AX
  ENGLAND
  ✍ British branch of the International Association of Crime Writers.

Independent Mystery Booksellers Association

Maryelizabeth Hart, Director — WEBSITE — www.mysterybooksellers.com
c/o Mysterious Galaxy — EMAIL — publicity@mystgalaxy.com
7051 Clairemont Mesa Blvd Ste 302
San Diego CA 92111-1040 USA
  ✍ Trade association for mutual support and promotion of specialty mystery booksellers. Gives the **Dilys Award** annually to the book "most fun to sell."

Independent Mystery Publishers

EMAIL — IMPrints@mysterypublishers.com
WEBSITE — www.mysterypublishers.com
  ✍ Informal group of small presses specializing in mystery. E-mail discussion list. Peri-
odically issues joint catalog of current releases, called *IMPrints*.

INTERNATIONAL ASSOCIATION OF CRIME WRITERS

Jeremiah Healy, President
186 Commonwealth Ave #31
Boston MA 02116-2751 USA

FAX 1-617-927-7520
EMAIL jeremiahealy@earthlink.net

➤ IACW, also known as the Asociacion Internacional de Escritores Policiacos (AIEP). To promote communication among writers & encourage translation. Members in 22 countries. Annual conference.

INTERNATIONAL ASSOCIATION OF CRIME WRITERS NA

Mary Frisque, Exec. Director
PO Box 8674
New York NY 10116-8674 USA

PHONE 1-212-243-8966
FAX 1-815-361-1477
EMAIL mfrisque@igc.org

➤ North American branch of IACW, including US and Canada. To promote communication among published crime writers worldwide. Gives the **Hammett Prize**. Newsletter: *Border Patrol.*

☞ INTERNATIONAL SISTER FIDELMA SOCIETY

David Robert Wooten
PO Box 1899
Little Rock AR 72203-1899 USA

EMAIL davidwu10@sbcglobal.net
WEBSITE www.sisterfidelma.com

✩ Fans of the series by Peter Tremayne, which features a 7th century Irish nun who is also a trained advocate of the Brehon law system. Journal *The Brehon* 3 times yearly.

THE JAMES HILTON SOCIETY

John Hammond, Chairman
49 Beckingthorpe Dr
Bottesford, Nottingham NG13
    0DN ENGLAND

✩ To promote interest in the life and work of novelist and scriptwriter James Hilton (1900–1954), author of *Murder at School* and other detective stories. Quarterly newsletter.

THE JOHN BUCHAN SOCIETY

Kenneth Hillier, Secretary
'Greenmantle', Main Street
Kings Newton
Melbourne, Derbyshire DE73 1BX
    ENGLAND

PHONE +44 1332 865315
EMAIL kah@greenmantle63.freeserve.co.uk
WEBSITE www.johnbuchansociety.co.uk

✩ Annual general meeting and dinner. Publishes the twice-yearly *John Buchan Journal.* Complete, searchable Buchan bibliography at website includes reviews of many titles.

MALICE DOMESTIC, LTD

PO Box 31137
Bethesda MD 20824-1137 USA

EMAIL info@malicedomestic.org
WEBSITE www.malicedomestic.org

➤ Non-profit organization to promote the traditional mystery. Sponsors annual **Malice Domestic** conference, contests, and grants for unpublished writers. Quarterly newsletter *The Usual Suspects*, free to conference attendees or by subscription.

THE MALTESE FALCON SOCIETY OF JAPAN

Toshihiko Taniguchi, Sec.
1-5-6 Kanda-surugadai, #207
Chiyoda-ku, Tokyo 101-0062 JAPAN

PHONE +81 3-3295-7335
WEBSITE www.asahi-net.or.jp/~AP9T-AMN/whatsmfs.html

⚓ Hardboiled/private eye fan club, monthly newsletter. Awards the **Falcon** to best hardboiled novel each year. Website in Japanese.

THE MARGERY ALLINGHAM SOCIETY

Mrs. Pamela Bruxner
2B Hiham Green
Winchelsea, East Sussex TN36 4HB
ENGLAND

PHONE +44 1797 222363
WEBSITE www.margeryallingham.fsnet.co.uk

☆ Est. 1988. For fans of Albert Campion et al. Annual dinner, trips. Patron: Joyce Allingham. Semiannual newsletter, *The Bottle Street Gazette.*

THE MEN WITH THE TWISTED KONJO

Hirayama Yuichi, BSI
2-10-12 Kamirenjaku
Mitaka-shi, Tokyo 181-0012 JAPAN

PHONE +81 422-43-2914
FAX +81 422-41-4735
EMAIL hirayama@parkcity.ne.jp
WEBSITE www.parkcity.ne.jp/~hirayama/index.htm

§ International Sherlock Holmes Society. Publishes the *Shoso-in Bulletin* (in English). Website in English and Japanese.

MURDER MUST ADVERTISE

Jeff Marks, Moderator

WEBSITE www.MurderMustAdvertise.com
WEBSITE groups.yahoo.com/group/MurderMustAdvertise/

⊘ Electronic discussion group for published mystery authors to trade ideas about book promotion. Publishers, booksellers, and publicists also welcome.

MYSTERY READERS INTERNATIONAL

Janet A Rudolph, Director
PO Box 8116
Berkeley CA 94707-8116 USA

EMAIL whodunit@murderonthemenu.com
WEBSITE www.mysteryreaders.org

⚓ Largest in the world—members in 50 states & 22 countries with local reading groups. Quarterly magazine *Mystery Readers Journal.*

MYSTERY WOMEN

c/o Ayo Onatade
137 Sandstone Rd
Grove Park
London SE12 0UT ENGLAND

PHONE +44 208 851 2293
EMAIL lizzie@calledbooks.demon.co.uk
WEBSITE www.mysterywomen.freeserve.co.uk
EMAIL ayoonatade@yahoo.com

⚓ UK crime fiction readers' group. Meets approx. every six weeks, with guest author speakers and/or book discussion (location varies). Newsletter 8 times a year, plus annual reading list. Website has news, reviews, interviews, and upcoming events.

MYSTERY WRITERS FORUM

Lauri Hart	PHONE/FAX	1-650-328-6828
111 Baywood Ave	EMAIL	lhart@zott.com
Menlo Park CA 94025-2701 USA	WEBSITE	www.MysteryWritersForum.com

⌀ Essential online resource for the mystery writer (published or unpublished), with threaded discussions on many topics.

MYSTERY WRITERS OF AMERICA

Margery Flax, Office Manager	PHONE	1-212-888-8171
17 E 47th St Fl 6	FAX	1-212-888-8107
New York NY 10017-1920 USA	EMAIL	mwa@mysterywriters.org
	WEBSITE	www.mysterywriters.org

⋟ Est. 1945 to promote the mystery genre and the interests of mystery writers. Ten regional chapters. Gives the **Edgar Allan Poe Awards** to recognize mystery fiction and related non-fiction in all media. Monthly newsletter *The Third Degree.*

NGAIO MARSH SOCIETY INTERNATIONAL

Nicole St John	EMAIL	johnstonstjohn@worldnet.att.net
103 Godwin Ave #299	WEBSITE	www.chipmunkcrossing.com/
Midland Park NJ 07432-1864 USA		activities/nmsi.html

☆ Est. 1996 to celebrate the life and work of Dame Edith Ngaio Marsh (1895–1982). Semi-annual newsletter, *Harmony,* annual journal, *Promptbook.* Publishes articles relating to Marsh's life and works, and presents awards in Marsh's memory at irregular intervals.

NIHON SUIRI SAKKA KYOKAI

Goh Ohsaka, Director	PHONE	+81 3-3401-3946
4-18-3 Minami Aoyama, #305	FAX	+81 3-3401-3235
Minato-ku, Tokyo 107-0062 JAPAN	WEBSITE	www.mystery.or.jp

⋟ Mystery Writers of Japan, Inc. Writers, critics, readers, & editors. Formerly Tantei Sakka Club (Detective Writers Club), est. 1947. Monthly newsletter.

OZSAINT

Ian Golledge, Hon. Sec.	EMAIL	i.golledge@qut.edu.au
2/9 Bedser St	WEBSITE	users.hunterlink.net.au/~lmcvd/
MacGregor QLD 4109 AUSTRALIA		saint/saint.htm

☆ Australian branch of **The Saint Club.**

POLICE WRITERS CLUB

LeslyeAnn Rolik	PHONE/FAX	1-703-723-4740
PO Box 738	EMAIL	leslye@policewriter.com
Ashburn VA 20146 USA	WEBSITE	www.policewriter.com

⋟ Helps both police officers and civilians get their police-related writing published. Newsletter *The Police Writer* includes markets, members news & writers tips. Annual conference.

PRIVATE EYE WRITERS OF AMERICA

Robert J Randisi
4342H Forest Deville Dr
Saint Louis MO 63129-1833 USA

PHONE 1-314-892-2623
EMAIL rrandisi@aol.com

☞ To promote fiction writing about professional investigators who are not employed by the goverment. Fans may join as associates. Presents annual **Shamus Awards** and sponsors periodic conference **EyeCon**. Quarterly newsletter, *Reflections in a Private Eye.*

RAYMOND CHANDLER GESELLSCHAFT

William R Adamson
Heidenheimer Str 106
89075 Ulm GERMANY

PHONE +49 731 205 3606
EMAIL william.adamson@zsp.uni-ulm.de

☞ Raymond Chandler Society of Germany. Awards the **Marlowe** for the best German and International crime novels.

REC.ARTS.MYSTERY

NEWSGROUP rec.arts.mystery

⌂ Online discussion forum for mystery lovers.

REICHENBACH IRREGULARS

Roger Bieman
Dammstrasse 61
8702 Zollikon, Zürich
SWITZERLAND

EMAIL mgeisser@access.ch

§ Sherlock Holmes Society of Switzerland. Publishes the *Reichenbach Journal* and *The Young Swiss Messenger.*

RIVERTONKLUBBEN

Mariann Fugelsø Nilssen, Secretary
Erika Nissens gt 5
0480 Oslo NORWAY

EMAIL mariann.f.nilssen@bokklubbene.no

☞ Crime Writers Association of Norway.

RWA MYSTERY/SUSPENSE CHAPTER

Amy Leitman, Membership Chair
PO Box 430758
Miami FL 33243 USA

WEBSITE www.rwamysterysuspense.org
EMAIL AmyWritesRomance@aol.com

☞ Special interest chapter of Romance Writers of America. Offers online workshops, discussion groups, and critique services. Bimonthly newsletter *The Kiss of Death.*

THE SAINT CLUB

Ian Dickerson, Hon. Sec.
Shandy St, Stepney
London E1 4ST ENGLAND

EMAIL club@saint.org
WEBSITE www.saint.org
WEBSITE www.simontemplar.tv

☆ For people interested in "the work of Simon Templar and the adventures of Leslie Charteris." Irregular newsletter, *The Epistle,* and merchandise available.

SAINTS AND SINNERS

Barbara Skoglund
1969 Price Ave
Maplewood MN 55109-4709 USA

PHONE 1-651-748-9771
EMAIL barbara.skoglund@att.net

☞ Twin Cities mystery reading group. Meets monthly at Roseville branch of Ramsey County Library. Frequently has author guests.

SÄLLSKAPET DECKARVÄNNERNA

Krister Nilsson
Box 2077
121 12 Johanneshov SWEDEN

☞ Society of Mystery Lovers. Est. 1975. For readers, writers, and critics.

SHERLOCK HOLMES' CHINESE SOCIETY

Henry P Cheng, President
138-15 63rd Ave
Flushing NY 11367 USA

PHONE/FAX 1-718-762-8765
EMAIL hpcheng@zdnetonebox.com

§ Est. 1996. International organization for readers of Sherlock Holmes.

SHERLOCK HOLMES KLUBBEN I DANMARK

Bjarne Nielsen, President
c/o Sherlock Holmes Museet
Egebjergvej 210
Strandhuse
4500 Nykøbing Sjælland DENMARK

PHONE +45 5932 9238
EMAIL sherlockiana@nielsen.mail.dk
WEBSITE www.sherlockiana.net/shklub/

§ The Danish Baker Street Irregulars. Est. 1950. Has annual meeting in January. Newsletter *Sherlockiana* 2 or 3 times yearly. Website in English and Danish.

THE SHERLOCK HOLMES SOCIETY OF LONDON

R J Ellis, Membership Secretary
13 Crofton Ave
Orpington, Kent BR6 8DU
ENGLAND

PHONE/FAX +44 1689 811314
EMAIL SHSL221b@aol.com
WEBSITE www.sherlock-holmes.org.uk

§ Largest Sherlockian Society in England. Publishes *The Sherlock Holmes Journal* semi-annually, and *The District Messenger*, a monthly newsletter, which is also available online. Extensive website. Founded as the Sherlock Holmes Society in 1934.

SHORT MYSTERY FICTION SOCIETY

Earl Staggs, President

EMAIL earl3429@aol.com
WEBSITE groups.yahoo.com/group/
Shortmystery/

⌀ Est. 1996 to recognize, promote, and support the creative art of short mysteries. Online discussion group. Gives annual **Derringer Awards**.

SISTERS IN CRIME

Beth Wasson
PO Box 442124
Lawrence KS 66044-8933 USA

EMAIL sistersincrime@juno.com
WEBSITE www.sistersincrime.org

☞ SinC. To support and educate others about the work of women mystery writers. Quarterly newsletter. Publishes guide to self-promotion for authors and annual list of books in print by members.

SISTERS IN CRIME AUSTRALIA

GPO Box 5319 BB
Melbourne VIC 3001 AUSTRALIA

EMAIL sincoz@hotmail.com
WEBSITE home.vicnet.net.au/~sincoz/

☞ Newsletter 3 times yearly. Gives **Scarlet Stiletto Award** and the **Davitt**. Est. 1991. Not affiliated with Sisters in Crime, US.

SOCIÉTÉ SHERLOCK HOLMES DE FRANCE

Alexis Barquin, Sec.
26, Avenue de la République
75011 Paris FRANCE

PHONE +33 1 4355 9676
WEBSITE www.sshf.com

§ Members hold an annual meeting of the entire society and frequent local meetings. Several periodicals and publications, extensive website. Electronic discussion list. Foreign members welcome. Est. 1993.

THE SOCIETY OF PHANTOM FRIENDS

Kate Emberg
PO Box 1437
North Highlands CA 95660-1437
USA

WEBSITE www.nancydrewsleuth.com/tww.html

☞ Fans and collectors of girls' series books, such as Nancy Drew, Judy Bolton, et al. Newsletter *The Whispered Watchword* 10/year. Annual conference "Phantom Friends Reunion." Authors of *The Girls' Series Companion*. Unofficial website has more information.

SOCIETY OF SEDENTARY SLEUTHS

Julee Johnson

EMAIL shpcny@clarityconnect.com

☞ Mystery readers group in central New York (Syracuse). Monthly meetings. New members welcome.

STIEG TRENTERS VÄNNER

Bertil Widerberg
Box 19
161 26 Bromma SWEDEN

PHONE +46 8 265 652
FAX +46 8 262 736

☆ Stieg Trenters Friends. Est. 1983 to honor one of Sweden's leading mystery writers.

SUOMEN DEKKARISEURA

PL 6
00551 Helsinki FINLAND

FAX +358 9 0205 811 288
EMAIL keijo.kettunen@kolumbus.fi
WEBSITE www.dekkariseura.fi

≶ The Finnish Whodunnit Society. Founded 1984. Quarterly publication *Ruumiin Kulttuuri*. Awards **Clue of the Year** to best crime novel or to best achievement related to the field. Website in English and Finnish. Accessories for sale at website.

SVENSKA DECKARAKADEMIN

Göran Bengtson, President
Bryggargatan 6 B, 1 tr
111 21 Stockholm SWEDEN

PHONE/FAX +46 8 248708

≶ Swedish Crime and Mystery Academy. 25 elected members in 2000. Novelists, critics, bibliographers, and collectors. Annual **Martin Beck Awards** for Swedish original and for translation.

DAS SYNDIKAT

c/o Reinhard Jahn
Breslauer Str. 10
Essen 45145 GERMANY

PHONE +49 201 765 699
EMAIL 100740.3540@compuserve.com
WEBSITE www.das-syndikat.com

≶ Autorengruppe Deutschsprachige Kriminalliteratur: German Crime Writers' Association. Est. 1986. Publication is *Secret Service*. Awards the **Glauser** & **Ehrenglauser**. Website has lots of German mystery news and links.

VHA: VON HERDER AIRGUNS, LTD.

Michael Ross
Postfach 42 06 70
50900 Köln GERMANY

PHONE/FAX +49 221 475 8063
WEBSITE von-herder.home.pages.de

§ German Sherlock Holmes Society, est. 1988. Annual meeting and regional get-togethers. Semiannual journal *SNOB: The Soft-Nosed Bullet-in*, electronic newsletter *The Striking (T)Rifles*, both in German.

THE VIDOCQ SOCIETY

1704 Locust St Fl 2
Philadelphia PA 19103-6107 USA

PHONE 1-215-545-1450
FAX 1-215-545-1773
EMAIL general@vidocq.org
WEBSITE www.vidocq.org

≶ International society of forensic experts and others, est. 1990, who volunteer their skills to investigate long-unsolved homicides. Journal (approx. 5/yr) available by subscription.

WILKIE COLLINS SOCIETY

Paul Lewis, Membership Secretary
4 Ernest Gardens
Chiswick, London W4 3QU
ENGLAND

EMAIL paul@deadline.demon.co.uk
WEBSITE www.gasson.demon.co.uk/wcs.html

☆ International society to promote interest in life and works of this author. Publishes a newsletter, an annual journal, & occasionally out-of-print Collins works. Est. 1980.

THE WOLFE PACK

Mary A Glascock
PO Box 822 Ansonia Station
New York NY 10023-9998 USA

EMAIL glascock@panix.com
WEBSITE www.nerowolfe.org

☆ Nero Wolfe fan club. Semiannual journal, *The Gazette*. Gives the **Nero Wolfe Award**. Shad Roe dinner (spring) & Black Orchid banquet (December). Local chapters are called racemes.

Events

AZ Murder Goes...

📖 Occasional symposium, sponsored by **The Poisoned Pen** bookstore, that explores a particular area or subgenre of crime fiction. No event in 2003.

Bare Bones Writers Retreat

J Miyoko Hensley
PO Box 86910
San Diego CA 92138-6910 USA

PHONE 1-760-753-0047
EMAIL mhensley@utm.net

📖 **Mar 28–30, 2003.** Biennial spring conference for mystery writers, sponsored by Sisters in Crime San Diego. Inexpensive, rustic campsite setting in Julian, CA. Well-known speakers. Est. 1994.

Bloody Words

Barbara Fradkin, Registrar
40 Glendenning Dr
Nepean ON K2H 7Y9 Canada

EMAIL info@bloodywords.com
WEBSITE www.bloodywords.com

📖 **Jun 13–15, 2003.** "Cops and Quills." 5th annual Canadian Mystery Conference at the Lord Elgin Hotel in downtown Ottawa. Guests of honour Howard Engel and Eric Wright, international guest of honour Val McDermid, toastmaster Mary Jane Maffini.

Book Passage Mystery Writers' Conference

Sarah Wingfield
51 Tamal Vista Blvd
Corte Madera CA 94925-1145 USA

PHONE 1-415-927-0960
FAX 1-415-924-3838
TOLLFREE 1-800-999-7909
EMAIL conferences@bookpassage.com
WEBSITE www.bookpassage.com

📖 **July 17–20, 2003.** Annual summer conference for mystery writers. Intensive program of workshops and lectures from successful authors, publishers, agents, and forensic experts. Small student to faculty ratio and lunches with faculty every day. Optional individual manuscript consultations.

Bouchercon 2003

Deen Kogan
c/o Society Hill Playhouse
507 S 8th St
Philadelphia PA 19147-1325 USA

PHONE 1-215-923-0211
FAX 1-215-923-1789
WEBSITE BconVegas2003.org
EMAIL shp@erols.com
EMAIL DeenKogan@NovelHost.net

📖 **Oct 16–19, 2003.** 34th annual World Mystery Convention, at the Riviera Hotel in Las Vegas, Nevada. Guests of Honor: US, James Lee Burke; Int'l, Ian Rankin; Body of Work, Ruth Rendel; Toastmaster, Lee Child; Contribution to the Field, Janet Hutchings; Fans, Ann & Jeff Smith. **Oct 15—**Writing Workshop, registration limited.

☛ BOUCHERCON 2004

Al Navis, Chair	PHONE	1-905-764-2665
c/o Almark & Co--Booksellers	FAX	1-905-764-5571
PO Box 7	EMAIL	almark-co@rogers.com
Thornhill ON L3T 3N1 CANADA	WEBSITE	www.almarkco.com

📁 Fall, 2004. Toronto, Ontario.

☛ BOUCHERCON 2005

Sonya Rice & Deen Kogan,	EMAIL	BCon2005@Book-Me.net
Co-Chairs	WEBSITE	Bouchercon.net

📁 Fall, 2005. Chicago, Illinois.

☛ BOUCHERCON 2006

Mary Helen Becker & Al Abramson,	EMAIL	Info@Bouchercon.com
Co-Chairs	WEBSITE	Bouchercon.com

📁 Fall, 2006. Madison, Wisconsin.

☛ BOUCHERCON 2007

Dana Stabenow, Chair	EMAIL	dana@stabenow.com

📁 Fall, 2007. Anchorage, Alaska.

BRITISH MYSTERY & CRIME WRITERS PROGRAM: LONDON AND OXFORD

Kathy Ackley	PHONE	1-715-346-3897
UWSP Extension 032 Main	FAX	1-715-346-3504
2100 Main St	EMAIL	kackley@kconline.com
Stevens Point WI 54481-3897 USA	WEBSITE	www.uwsp.edu/extension/ NonCredit/travel/

📁 **Aug 21–Sep 8, 2003.** London/Oxford tour. Talks by UK crime writers, *The Mousetrap,* private reception at Crime in Store, tea in Kate Charles's garden, attendance at St. Hilda's Crime & Mystery Weekend. Academic credit available.

CAPE FEAR CRIME FESTIVAL

Nicki Leone	PHONE	1-910-256-4490
1908 Eastwood Rd Suite 116	FAX	1-910-256-4770
Wilmington NC 28403-7234 USA	WEBSITE	www.galleone.com/cfcf.htm
	EMAIL	buyer@bristolbooks.com

📁 **Oct 31–Nov 2, 2003.** Keynote speaker Carolyn Hart; Guest of Honor Carole Nelson Douglas. Wilmington NC festival includes author readings, book signings, panel discussions, evening readings and morning brunches, and a Halloween tour of a historic and possibly haunted cemetery. Est. 2001.

CHESTER HIMES MYSTERY WRITERS CONFERENCE

The Friends of Chester Himes	PHONE	1-415-885-4709
PO Box 3065	EMAIL	tfoch2000@yahoo.com
Oakland CA 94618 USA		

📁 **May 16–17, 2003.** Annual conference since 1996. A daylong presentation of panels, individual papers and film, focusing on African-American mystery writers. At Oakland Museum of California. Gives the **Chester Himes Mystery Awards.**

CLUEFEST 12

Caryl Thompson   PHONE/FAX   1-972-669-9932
Con & Dagger Productions   EMAIL   ClueFest@aol.com
604 Vernet St   WEBSITE   hometown.aol.com/cluefest/
Richardson TX 75080-4232 USA   Cluefest.html

Jul 18–20, 2003. Annual mystery readers book fair in Dallas area. Guests of Honor are G.M. Ford, Tony Fennelly, and Bill Crider (Fan Guest of Honor).

COLORADO GOLD WRITERS CONFERENCE

Diana Rowe Martinez   PHONE   1-303-331-2608
Rocky Mountain Fiction Writers   EMAIL   conference@rmfw.org
PO Box 260244   WEBSITE   www.rmfw.org
Denver CO 80226-0244 USA

Sep 13–15, 2003. Annual fall conference sponsored by Rocky Mountain Fiction Writers. Includes significant mystery track. Writing contest open to all.

COZY CRIMES, CREAM TEAS & BOOKS, BOOKS, BOOKS ·

Jan Dean   PHONE   1-228-255-6923
8340 Makiki Dr   EMAIL   jandean@bellsouth.net
Diamondhead MS 39525 USA

Sep 3–14, 2003. St Hilda's Crime & Mystery Weekend in Oxford plus East Anglia & London. Twelve-day tours to the UK to meet mystery authors, visit scenic areas, enjoy elegant teas, and bookshop in Hay-on-Wye, Wigtown, and other bookish places.

CRIME SCENE

National Film Theatre   WEBSITE   www.bfi.org.uk
Belvedere Rd, South Bank
Waterloo, London SE1 8XT
   ENGLAND

Annual July film festival, plus panels, discussions, etc. Sponsored by the British Film Institute. Est. 2000.

DIE CRIMINALE

                          EMAIL   criminale@westerwald.info
                          WEBSITE   www.die-criminale.de

May 14–18, 2003. Westerwald. Annual meeting of **Das Syndikat**, the German Crime Writers Association. Discussions, readings, panels. Open to the public.

DAPHNE DU MAURIER FESTIVAL OF ARTS AND LITERATURE

Restormel Borough Council   PHONE   +44 1726 223439
39 Penwinnick Rd   EMAIL   paulwarbey@restormel.fsnet.co.uk
St. Austell, Cornwall PL25 5DR   WEBSITE   www.restormel.gov.uk/daphne/
   ENGLAND

May 9–18, 2003. Annual festival, est. 1998. Guided walks, exhibitions, talks by leading writers, free entertainment and "star names." In & around Fowey on the "Cornish Riviera."

DEAD ON DEANSGATE

Dave Lovely, Crime Fiction Buyer	PHONE	+44 161 832 1992
91 Deansgate	FAX	+44 161 835 1534
Manchester M3 2BW ENGLAND	EMAIL	enquiries@manchester-deansgate.waterstones.co.uk
	WEBSITE	www.waterstones.co.uk

Annual October conference in Manchester, England, since 1998. Sponsored by Waterstone's Deansgate with the support of the **Crime Writers Association.** No decision yet on holding an event in 2003.

DEADLY INK MYSTERY CONFERENCE

Patricia Biringer	PHONE	1-973-627-2806
15 Mohawk Ave	EMAIL	pab@nac.net
Rockaway NJ 07866-1805 USA	WEBSITE	www.deadlyink.com

Jun 13–14, 2003. Small, friendly annual conference in Parsippany, NJ. Two panels to choose from on Friday night plus Deadly Dessert Party; continental breakfast, ten workshops/panels to choose from, and grand banquet lunch on Saturday. Book room and book signings. To receive a brochure please send email giving your postal address.

FESTIVAL DU ROMAN NOIR

Hôtel de Ville BP 308	EMAIL	pv@polar-frontignan.org
34113 Frontignan FRANCE	WEBSITE	www.polar-frontignan.org

Annual summer celebration of crime fiction, with French, Spanish, and English authors. Five days, many events, discussions, films, and performances. Sponsored by the city of Frontignan la Peyrade and the organization Soleil Noir. Since 1998.

☛ FESTIVAL OF MYSTERY

c/o Mystery Lovers Bookshop	PHONE	1-412-828-4877
514 Allegheny River Blvd	FAX	1-412-828-6470
Oakmont PA 15139-1617 USA	TOLLFREE	1-888-800-6078
	EMAIL	mysterylovers@mysterylovers.com
	WEBSITE	www.mysterylovers.com

May 5, 2003. Sponsored by Mystery Lovers Bookshop, this annual festival following Malice Domestic brings 30 authors and several hundred fans together for an evening of talks and signings. Full details at the website.

FLATIRONS BLUNT INSTRUMENTS

Thora E Chinnery	PHONE	1-303-499-0203
c/o SinC, Rocky Mountain Chapter	EMAIL	chinnery@chisp.net
PO Box 19846		
Boulder CO 80308 USA		

Jun 14, 2003. Annual summer mystery writers and readers workshop in Boulder, Colorado. Sponsored by Rocky Mountain Chapter of Sisters in Crime. Est. 1996.

HARRIETTE AUSTIN WRITERS CONFERENCE

Charles Connor, Program Director   PHONE   1-706-542-1585
University of Georgia   FAX   1-413-622-8007
G-9 Aderhold   TOLLFREE   1-800-884-1381
Athens GA 30602-7101 USA   EMAIL   hawc@coe.uga.edu
   WEBSITE   www.coe.uga.edu//hawc/

📖 **Jul 18–19, 2003.** Annual conference since 1994. Includes over 30 sessions with authors, editors, and agents, providing workshops on the craft of writing, getting published, and the writing life in a range of genres including mainstream fiction, & non-fiction, children & YA, inspirational, mystery and forensics. Expected attendance 425.

☞ HARROWGATE CRIME WRITERS FESTIVAL

   EMAIL   crime@harrogate-festival.org.uk
   WEBSITE   www.harrogate-festival.org.uk

📖 **Jul 17–20, 2003.** First launch of new event at established arts festival. Writers attending include Colin Dexter, Peter Robinson, Walter Mosley, Janet Evanovich, Ian Rankin, and Val McDermid.

LEFT COAST CRIME 2003

Helen Howerton, Chairman   EMAIL   LCC2003@aol.com
13905 Giordano St   WEBSITE   www.LeftCoastCrime2003.com
La Puente CA 91746 USA

📖 **Feb 27–Mar 2, 2003.** "Lights, Camera, Murder!" Pasadena, California, at the Hilton Pasadena. Guest of Honor Robert Crais, Fan Guest of Honor Sue Feder, Toastmaster Jerrilyn Farmer.

☞ LEFT COAST CRIME 2004

Bill & Toby Gottfried, Co-Chairs   EMAIL   lcc2004@gottfried.org
registration: WEBSITE   www.lcc2004.com
c/o Noemi Levine
2625 Alcatraz Ave #332
Berkeley CA 94705 USA

📖 **Feb 19–22, 2004.** Monterey, California. "Time and Tide Wait for No Body." Author Guests of Honor: Sharan Newman and Walter Mosley; Lifetime Achievement: Dick Lupoff; Toastmistress: Gillian Roberts; Fan Guests of Honor: Bryan Barrett & Thom Walls.

☞ LOVE IS MURDER

Continuing Education Dept   PHONE   1-630-942-2208
College of DuPage   EMAIL   loveismurder@cdnet.cod.edu
425 Fawell Blvd   EMAIL   Kanarh@cdnet.cod.edu
Glen Ellyn IL 60137-6599 USA   WEBSITE   www.cod.edu/ComConEd/murder/

📖 **Feb 7–9, 2003.** Annual conference focusing on mystery and suspense (romantic and otherwise). Panel discussions and workshops. Sponsored by College of DuPage and held at Oak Brook Marriott Hotel.

MAGNA CUM MURDER

Kathryn Kennison, Coordinator   PHONE   1-765-285-8975
Ball State University   FAX   1-765-747-9566
E B & Bertha C Ball Center   EMAIL   kennisonk@aol.com
Muncie IN 47306-0001 USA   WEBSITE   www.magnacummurder.com

Oct 24–26, 2003. Mid America Crime Fiction Festival. Guest of Honor Jeffery Deaver. Annual conference for scholars, fans & writers, est. 1994. Newsletter **Pomp & Circumstantial Evidence.**

MALICE DOMESTIC XV

703 Kenbrook Dr   EMAIL   registrar@malicedomestic.org
Silver Spring MD 20902-3224 USA   WEBSITE   www.malicedomestic.org

May 2–4, 2003. Guest of Honor Barbara D'Amato, Toastmaster Parnell Hall, Lifetime Achievement Award Elizabeth Peters (Barbara Michaels, Barbara Mertz), Fan Guest of Honor Donna Beatley, and Ghost of Honor Agatha Christie. Annual conference in Washington DC area to celebrate the traditional mystery. Gives **Agatha Awards.**

MAYHEM IN THE MIDLANDS

Jennifer Kirchmann   PHONE   1-402-444-4828
Omaha Public Library   EMAIL   jennk@omaha.lib.ne.us
215 S 15th St   EMAIL   sallyfellows1@cox.net
Omaha NE 68102-1601 USA   WEBSITE   www.omaha.lib.ne.us/mayhem/

May 29–Jun 1, 2003. Annual conference, est. 2000; sponsored by Omaha Public Library and Lincoln City Libraries. Guest of Honor Jan Burke; Toastmaster Jerrilyn Farmer.

MID-ATLANTIC MYSTERY BOOK FAIR & CONVENTION

Deen Kogan   PHONE   1-215-923-0211
c/o Society Hill Playhouse   FAX   1-215-923-1789
507 S 8th St   WEBSITE   midatlanticmystery.org
Philadelphia PA 19147-1325 USA   EMAIL   shp@erols.com
   EMAIL   DeenKogan@NovelHost.net

Fall 2004. Annual event, est. 1990, sponsored by **Detecto Mysterioso** booksellers. (No event in 2003, as sponsors are producing Bouchercon this year.)

MURDER AHOY

Elaine Raco Chase   PHONE/FAX   1-703-378-9580
4333 Majestic Ln   EMAIL   simplycruises@aol.com
Fairfax VA 22033-3500 USA   EMAIL   elainerc@juno.com

Mar 6–13, 2004. Mystery Writers & Readers Conference at Sea. Keynote speaker best-selling thriller writer Catherine Coulter. Also leading financial crime investigator Ed Pankou.

Murder in the Grove

Genesis Kohler   PHONE   1-208-322-2788
Borders Books & Music   EMAIL   gkohler@bordersstores.com
1123 N Milwaukee St   WEBSITE   www.sistersincrimeboise.org
Boise ID 83704-8474 USA

📅 **May 30–31, 2003.** Annual writers & readers conference (est. 1998) at the Grove Hotel, Boise. Keynote author: Michael Connelly. Suspense author Ridley Pearson will present Governor's Ridley Award. Sponsored by Boise Chapter of Sisters in Crime.

☛ Murder in the Magic City

     EMAIL   heidi@heidimoos.com
     WEBSITE   webpages.charter.net/
     southernsisters/conference.html

📅 **Feb 8, 2003.** Birmingham, Alabama's first mystery conference, sponsored by Southern Sisters in Crime. Guests of Honor Lee Child and Meg Chittenden. All-day conference includes author panels, book signings, lunch and interviews.

☛ Mystery Series Week

c/o Purple Moon Press   EMAIL   info@mysteryseriesweek.com
3319 Greenfield Rd, #317   WEBSITE   www.mysteryseriesweek.com
Dearborn MI 48120-1212 USA

📅 **Oct 5–11, 2003.** Celebrates continuing characters in detective fiction with special library and bookstore events during the first full week in October. Est. 1998. Sponsored by **Purple Moon Press.**

No Crime Unpublished™

Judith K Smith, Coordinator   EMAIL   jks18@aol.com
PO Box 251646   WEBSITE   www.sistersincrimela.com
Los Angeles CA 90025-9263 USA

📅 **Jun 1, 2003.** Biannual one-day conference with workshops led by established writers. Open to members and non-members. See website for details.

☛ NYC Collectible Paperback & Pulp Fiction Expo

Gary Lovisi   PHONE   1-718-646-6126
PO Box 209   EMAIL   orders@gryphonbooks.com
Brooklyn NY 11228-0209 USA   WEBSITE   www.gryphonbooks.com

📅 **Sep 7, 2003.** 14th annual book show with many crime and mystery author guests, as well as many dealers specializing in scarce & out of print mystery & crime books. Holiday Inn, 440 W 57th St.

Of Dark and Stormy Nights

c/o Jeanne M Dams   EMAIL   jdams@JeanneDams.com
PO Box 6804   WEBSITE   www.zoss.com/stormynights
South Bend IN 46660-6804 USA

📅 **Jun 14, 2003.** Annual June one-day conference on writing mystery fiction & crime-related nonfiction, sponsored by MWA Midwest Chapter. Held in Rolling Meadows, Illinois (suburban Chicago). Est. 1982.

SEMANA NEGRA

c/o Paco Ignacio Taibo II	WEBSITE	www.semananegra.com
Atlixco 163A	EMAIL	marinataibo3@aol.com
Colonia Condesa DF 06140 MEXICO	EMAIL	marianataibo3@yahoo.com.mx

July, 2003. "Black Week" celebration of crime writing, held annually in Gijón, Spain, since 1988. Crowded with holiday makers, it includes all kinds of fiesta events such as rides and performances, as well as a book fair. Has its own train from Madrid, and its own newspaper. All events are open to the public.

SLEUTHFEST

c/o Anne K Walsh	PHONE	1-954-915-9684
6056 NW 56th Dr	EMAIL	Rwymer55@aol.com
Coral Springs FL 33067 USA	WEBSITE	www.sleuthfest.com

Mar 13–16, 2003. Special guests Sue Grafton & Dr. Henry Lee. Annual writers conference, est. 1994. Hilton Hotel, Deerfield Beach/Boca Raton, Florida. Sponsored by Florida chapter of MWA and Criminal Justice Institute of Broward Community College.

ST HILDA'S CRIME & MYSTERY WEEKEND

Eileen Roberts	PHONE	+44 1865 276867
St Hilda's College	FAX	+44 1865 276820
Cowley Place	EMAIL	eileen.roberts@st-
Oxford OX4 1DY ENGLAND		hildas.oxford.ac.uk

Sep 5–7, 2003. 10th anniversary of small, highly esteemed annual symposium, est. 1993. Attendees stay in college.

☞ WALLONIE 2003, ANNÉE SIMENON AU PAYS DE LIÈGE

12, rue des Prémonitrés	EMAIL	simenon2003@prov-lieg.be
4000 Liège BELGIUM	WEBSITE	www.simenon2003.be

☆ 2003. Year-long program of events honoring Georges Simenon in his hometown of Liège, Belgium, 100 years after his birth.

☞ WMU PRAGUE SUMMER PROGRAM: CRIME FICTION WORKSHOP

WMU Office of Study Abroad	EMAIL	prague@wmich.edu
B-200 Ellsworth Hall	EMAIL	eversz@mac.com
Kalamazoo MI 49008 USA	WEBSITE	www.wmich.edu/studyabroad/
		prague/cw.courses.html

Jun 28–Jul 27, 2003. Creative writing workshop with author Robert Eversz, in one of Europe's most beautiful (and inexpensive) cities. Classes three mornings per week; students may take either or both of two 2-week sessions. Academic credit from Western Michigan Univ.

Periodicals and Reviewers

DICK ADLER

1250 Amherst Ave #205
Los Angeles CA 90025-1148 USA

EMAIL   dickadler@excite.com

☞ Reviews for *Chicago Tribune, Publishers Weekly,* and several internet publications.

ALFRED HITCHCOCK'S MYSTERY MAGAZINE

Linda Landrigan, Editor
475 Park Ave S Fl 11
New York NY 10016-6901 USA

SUBSCRIBE   1-800-333-3311
WEBSITE   www.themysteryplace.com

AHMM. Eleven issues a year including one double issue. Short mystery fiction in all subgenres, logic problem, and Mysterious Photograph contest. "Booked and Printed" column reviews 6–8 mysteries each issue. Writer's guidelines at website.

☞ DIE ALLIGATORPAPIERE

NordPark Verlag
Klingelholl 53
42281 Wuppertal GERMANY

PHONE   +49 202 51 10 89
EMAIL   webmaster@nordpark-verlag.de
WEBSITE   www.alligatorpapiere.de

German-language webzine with news, reviews, interviews. German and international author biographies & bibliographies. Sponsored by publisher NordPark Verlag.

AUDIOFILE

Robin F Whitten, Editor/Publisher
37 Silver St
PO Box 109
Portland ME 04112-0109 USA

PHONE   1-207-774-7563
FAX   1-207-775-3744
TOLLFREE   1-800-506-1212
EMAIL   info@audiofilemagazine.com
WEBSITE   www.audiofilemagazine.com

"The Magazine for People Who Love Audiobooks." Bimonthly, reviews over 100 audiobooks each issue, with a regular column on mystery and suspense. Also interviews, resources, list of new releases.

THE BAKER STREET DISPATCH

Thomas Biblewski, Editor
PO Box 5503
Toledo OH 43613-0503 USA

EMAIL   biblejt@aol.com

§ Perhaps the largest Sherlock Holmes newsletter, bimonthly since 1990. Includes an insightful glimpse into the stories, a book or movie review, a calendar of events, plus more.

THE BAKER STREET JOURNAL

Steven Rothman, Editor
220 W Rittenhouse Sq #15-D
Philadelphia PA 19103 USA

EMAIL   email@bakerstreetjournal.com
WEBSITE   www.bakerstreetjournal.com

§ Quarterly since 1946. "THE journal for those who follow Sherlock Holmes." Official publication of the **Baker Street Irregulars**. A CD-ROM of the first 50 years of *BSJ*, fully indexed, is available; see website for details.

BILL CRIDER'S NEWSLETTER

1606 S Hill St	EMAIL	abc@BillCrider.com
Alvin TX 77511-4356 USA	WEBSITE	www.BillCrider.com

ⅰ Send stamps. Alligator jokes, news items, & paraphernalia appreciated.

BLACK MASK MAGAZINE

Keith Alan Deutsch, Publisher	EMAIL	admin@blackmaskmagazine.com
Robert Preston, Editor-in-Chief	WEBSITE	www.blackmaskmagazine.com
26 Dixon Dr		
Woodbridge NJ 07095-2103 USA		

∅ Cyber-revival of the famous pulp magazine offers stories, reviews, reprints, posters, and a "center for the enjoyment and study of all forms of mass market popular American entertainment." Writers guidelines at website.

BOOK WORLD

Michael Dirda, Senior Editor	PHONE	1-202-334-7882
The Washington Post	WEBSITE	www.washingtonpost.com
1150 15th St NW		
Washington DC 20071-0002 USA		

☞ Weekly literary section of nationally-distributed metropolitan newspaper. Reviews 2000 books/yr.

BOOKLIST

Brad Hooper, Adult Books Editor	SUBSCRIBE	1-888-350-0949
American Library Assoc	EMAIL	bhooper@ala.org
50 E Huron St	WEBSITE	www.ala.org/booklist/
Chicago IL 60611-2795 USA		

subscription:
PO Box 607
Mt. Morris IL 61054-7564 USA

☞ Over 150 reviews/issue of adult books, 22 issues/year. Published by the American Library Association. Guidelines for book submission at the website.

BOOKPAGE

Lynn Green, Editor	PHONE	1-615-292-8926
ProMotion Inc	FAX	1-615-292-8249
2143 Belcourt Ave	TOLLFREE	1-800-726-4242
Nashville TN 37212-3503 USA	EMAIL	lynn@bookpage.com
	WEBSITE	www.bookpage.com

☞ A monthly general interest book review, designed to be distributed to readers as well as booksellers. Typically reviews 40 to 50 books each month.

CADS: Crime and Detective Stories

Geoff Bradley, Editor
9 Vicarage Hill
South Benfleet, Essex SS7 1PA
    England

PHONE	+44 1268 793338
EMAIL	Geoffcads@aol.com

 An irregular magazine of comment & criticism about crime and detective fiction. Articles, reviews, a wealth of detail. Essential reading for serious fans of the genre.

CDM: Short Stories of Crime, Detection & Mystery

Per Olaisen, Editor
Rådmansgatan 31 A
311 45 Falkenberg Sweden

PHONE	+46 8 508 601 10
EMAIL	perolaisen@yahoo.com
WEBSITE	www.expage.com/olaisen/

 Quarterly fiction magazine. Est. 1991. Stories in Swedish, English, Danish, Norwegian.

Cemetery Dance

Richard T Chizmar, Editor
PO Box 623
Forest Hill MD 21050 USA
subscription:
132B Industry Lane
Forest Hill MD 21050 USA

PHONE	1-410-558-5901
FAX	1-410-588-5904
EMAIL	info@cemeterydance.com
WEBSITE	www.cemeterydance.com

 "The Magazine of Horror, Dark Mystery, and Suspense." Bi-monthly (6/yr). Short fiction, interviews, articles, commentary, reviews. Subscriptions and back issues may be ordered on line.

Oline H Cogdill

Sun-Sentinel
200 E Las Olas Blvd Ste 1000
Fort Lauderdale FL 33301-2293 USA

PHONE	1-954-356-4675
FAX	1-954-356-4676
TOLLFREE	1-800-945-5182
EMAIL	OCogdill@sun-sentinel.com

 Reviews mysteries for *South Florida Sun-Sentinel* and Knight-Ridder-Tribune syndicate.

Cozies, Capers & Crimes

Geraldine Galentree
2510 Blyth Dr
Dallas TX 75228-5023 USA

PHONE	1-214-320-8226
FAX	1-214-319-7695
EMAIL	galentre@mail.airmail.net
WEBSITE	www.coziescapersandcrimes.com

 A monthly email newsletter for book lovers. Send name and email address with request to subscribe. Geraldine Galentree's reviews also appear in *Mystery News* and on various internet sources.

Crescent Blues

Jean Marie Ward
PO Box 3121
Arlington VA 22203 USA

EMAIL	crescentblues@hotmail.com
WEBSITE	www.crescentblues.com

 Slick e-zine with news, articles, reviews about mystery and other genres. No fiction.

CRIME FACTORY

David Honeybone, Editor	FAX	+61 3 9443 7943
c/o Preston Lower Post Office	EMAIL	editor@crimefactory.net
3 Gilbert Road	WEBSITE	www.crimefactory.net
Preston VIC 3072 AUSTRALIA		

ko Australian crime writing magazine covers the English-speaking world. News, interviews, articles, fiction, and true crime. Quarterly.

CRIME TIME

Barry Forshaw, Editor	PHONE	+44 1582 761 264
Oldcastle Books	FAX	+44 1582 712 244
PO Box 394	EMAIL	ct@crimetime.co.uk
Harpenden AL5 1XJ ENGLAND	EMAIL	yornstrand@yahoo.co.uk
	WEBSITE	www.crimetime.co.uk

ko CT. Quarterly. Est. 1995. A substantial trade paperback with features and reviews, interviews, news and information. Selected articles and reviews available at website.

CRIMESTALKER CASEBOOK

Andrew McAleer, Editor	PHONE	1-617-552-3726
121 Follen Rd		
Lexington MA 02421-5942 USA		

ko Short stories of "murder mystery, Gothic tales, and poetry noir."

CRIMEWAVE

Andy Cox, Editor	PHONE	+44 1353 777931
TTA Press	EMAIL	TTAPress@aol.com
5 Martins Lane, Witcham	WEBSITE	www.ttapress.com
Ely, Cambridgeshire CB6 2LB		
ENGLAND		

North American:
c/o Wayne Edwards
360 W 76th Ave #H
Anchorage AK 99518 USA

ko All fiction semiannual, with stories from well-known and unknown writers. Large paperback size, color, illustrated, 132 pages. Beautifully designed, excellent content.

DAST MAGAZINE

Bertil Falk, Editor	EMAIL	gondolin@swipnet.se
Box 20010	WEBSITE	www.keg.se/dast/
161 02 Bromma SWEDEN		

ko Detective, Agents, Science fiction, Thrillers. Quarterly in Swedish. International focus. Short stories, reviews, interviews, profiles, on collecting, upcoming releases. Est. 1968.

THE DEADLY DIRECTORY

Kate Derie, Editor
6702 N Casas Adobes Dr
Tucson AZ 85704-6124 USA

PHONE 1-520-742-6946
FAX 1-520-742-4179
EMAIL info@deadlyserious.com
WEBSITE www.deadlyserious.com

jj Annual directory of mystery booksellers, publications, organizations, conventions, events, related products & services.

DEADLY PLEASURES

George Easter, Editor
PO Box 969
Bountiful UT 84011-0969 USA

PHONE 1-801-294-7232
FAX 1-801-296-1993
WEBSITE www.deadlypleasures.com
EMAIL george@deadlypleasures.com

jj Quarterly magazine packed with articles, reviews, letters, news, etc. Includes UK as well as US releases. Est. 1993. Gives the **Barry Awards**.

☛ DETECTIVE MYSTERY STORIES

504 E Morris St
Seymour TX 76380-2212 USA

EMAIL fadingshadows@juno.com
WEBSITE www.geocities.com/
fadingshadows1/

jj Monthly fiction 'zine, digest size, approx 80 pp. Five or six stories per issue. Submission guidelines at website.

THE DROOD REVIEW OF MYSTERY

Jim Huang, Editor
484 E Carmel Dr #378
Carmel IN 46032-2812 USA

FAX 1-317-705-1402
EMAIL info@droodreview.com
WEBSITE www.droodreview.com

jj In-depth reviews of recent titles. Previews of all upcoming mystery titles. Bimonthly. Yearly editor's choice lists. Publishes books about mystery under the imprint **Crum Creek Press / Drood Review Books**.

ELLERY QUEEN'S MYSTERY MAGAZINE

Janet Hutchings, Editor
475 Park Ave S Fl 11
New York NY 10016-6901 USA

SUBSCRIBE 1-800-333-3053
WEBSITE www.themysteryplace.com

jj EQMM. "The World's Leading Mystery Magazine." Est. 1941. Short mystery fiction in all subgenres. Eleven issues a year including one double issue. Book review column "The Jury Box" reviews 8–10 mysteries each issue. Writer's guidelines at website.

FEMMES FATALES

Dean James, Editor

EMAIL thefatales@femmesfatalesauthors.com
WEBSITE FemmesFatalesAuthors.com

0 Semiannual newsletter featuring eight women mystery writers: Donna Andrews, Meg Chittenden, Charlaine Harris, Julie Wray Herman, Toni L.P. Kelner, D.R. Meredith, Marlys Millhiser, Kris Neri.

FIRSTS: THE BOOK COLLECTOR'S MAGAZINE

Robin Smiley, Publisher	PHONE	1-520-529-1355
PO Box 65166	FAX	1-520-529-5847
Tucson AZ 85728-5166 USA	EMAIL	firstsmag@aol.com
	WEBSITE	www.firsts.com

☎ Monthly. Frequent articles about mystery authors, annual special mystery issue. Interviews, profiles, upcoming releases. Collector's Calendar.

FOREWORD MAGAZINE

Alex Moore, Managing Editor	PHONE	1-231-933-3699
129-1/2 E Front St	FAX	1-231-933-3899
Traverse City MI 49684-2508 USA	EMAIL	alex@forewordmagazine.com
	WEBSITE	forewordmagazine.com

☎ Bimonthly journal. Reviews and articles focusing on independent and university presses. Wide distribution to librarians and booksellers, also available by subscription.

FUTURES MYSTERIOUS ANTHOLOGY MAGAZINE

Babs Lakey, Publisher	PHONE	1-612-724-4023
Earl Staggs, Fiction Editor	EMAIL	babs@fmam.biz
3039 38th Ave S	WEBSITE	www.fmam.biz
Minneapolis MN 55406-2140 USA		

☎ FMAM. Quarterly magazine features primarily mystery fiction. Contests, cartoons, mystery crossword. Publisher's Choice and Fire to Fly awards. "The Starting Line" (for new writers). Single copies and subscriptions for sale in online store.

GIALLO

c/o Kobunsha	EMAIL	honyaku@kobunsha.com
1-16-6 Otowa	WEBSITE	www.kobunsha.com/magazine/
Bunkoyo-ku, Tokyo 112-8790 JAPAN		giallo/

☎ Quarterly. Stories, columns, interviews. Successor to *EQ*.

THE GUMSHOE SITE

Jiro Kimura	PHONE	+81 76-263-4482
8-2 Hashiba-cho, #302	FAX	+81 76-263-4480
Kanazawa, Ishikawa JAPAN	EMAIL	jkimura@nsknet.or.jp
	WEBSITE	www.nsknet.or.jp/~jkimura/

⌨ Always the most current mystery news from a knowledgeable columnist for *Hayakawa's Mystery Magazine*.

HANDHELDCRIME

Victoria Esposito-Shea & Jamey	WEBSITE	www.handheldcrime.com
Dumas, Editors	EMAIL	victoria@handheldcrime.com
33 State St		
Canton NY 13617 USA		

⌨ Short mystery fiction, reviews, and articles, specially formatted for handhelds, delivered free of charge by e-mail, through AvantGo, or by download from the website.

HARDBOILED MAGAZINE

Gary Lovisi, Editor
PO Box 209
Brooklyn NY 11228-0209 USA

PHONE 1-718-646-6126
EMAIL orders@gryphonbooks.com
WEBSITE www.gryphonbooks.com

Hard, cutting edge fiction, by big-name pros and new writers. Now in trade paperback "double issue" format with 30-35 stories. Average 2 issues/yr. Est. 1988.

HAYAKAWA'S MYSTERY MAGAZINE

Hiroyuki Chida, Editor
c/o Hayakawa Publishing
2-2 Kanda-tacho
Chiyoda-ku, Tokyo 101-0046 JAPAN

PHONE +81 3-3252-3114
FAX +81 3-3252-3115
EMAIL KFG03025@nifty.ne.jp
WEBSITE www.hayakawa-online.co.jp

Monthly. Stories, columns, interviews.

R JOHN HAYES

52 Athabasca Ave
Devon AB T9G 1G6 CANADA

EMAIL liardrg@telusplanet.net

Writes a biweekly books column, which features mystery about 10 times a year, appearing in many newspapers in western Canada and north-central US.

I LOVE A MYSTERY

Sally Powers
13547 Ventura Blvd PMB 111
Sherman Oaks CA 91423-3825 USA

EMAIL sallypowers@earthlink.net
WEBSITE www.ILoveAMysteryNewsletter.com

Online-only newsletter with lots of mystery fiction reviews plus occasional bits of news and commentary.

IN A MELLOTONE

John Harvey
Garden Flat
71 Dartmouth Park Road
London NW5 1SL ENGLAND

PHONE/FAX +44 20 7485 4611
EMAIL slowdancer@mellotone.co.uk
WEBSITE www.mellotone.co.uk

The John Harvey/Charlie Resnick/Slow Dancer Press Newsletter. Twice yearly, free.

JANUARY MAGAZINE

J. Kingston Pierce, Crime Fiction
    Editor
146 N 78th St, Suite 1
Seattle WA 98103-4608 USA

FAX 1-206-782-3197
EMAIL jpwrites@sprynet.com
WEBSITE www.januarymagazine.com

The large Crime Fiction section of this attractive on-line magazine has well-written, in-depth reviews, interviews, and articles. Also available is a monthly email newsletter, "The Rap Sheet."

JOHN THORNDYKE'S JOURNAL

David Ian Chapman   EMAIL   dichapman9@aol.com
55 Highfield Gardens
Aldershot, Hampshire GU11 3DB
   ENGLAND
   ☆ Concerning author R. Austin Freeman.

JOURNAL OF CRIMINAL JUSTICE AND POPULAR CULTURE

Draper Hall #213   PHONE   1-518-442-5609
135 Western Ave   FAX   1-518-442-5716
Albany NY 12222-0001 USA   WEBSITE   www.albany.edu/scj/jcjpc/
                     EMAIL   sunycrj@cnsunix.albany.edu

   ௸ Scholarly research and opinion on the intersection of crime, criminal justice, and popular culture. Available online in both HTML and PDF. Sample article: "Striking Evidence: The Matchbook as a Cultural Artifact in Criminal Cases."

JURY

Bertil Widerberg, Editor   PHONE   +46 8 265 652
Box 19   FAX   +46 8 262 736
161 26 Bromma SWEDEN

   ௸ Quarterly, in Swedish but international scope, est. 1971. Articles, interviews, news, reviews, rarely short fiction. Annual list of all mystery books published in Swedish.

KIRKUS REVIEWS

Anne Larsen, Editor   PHONE   1-646-654-4602
770 Broadway   FAX   1-646-654-4706
New York NY 10003-9595 USA   EMAIL   kirkusrev@kirkusreviews.com
                     WEBSITE   www.kirkusreviews.com

   ☎ Semimonthly magazine with prepublication reviews of 6,000 books annually. Book submission guidelines at the website.

THE KISS OF DEATH

Patty Burns, Editor   PHONE   1-215-699-9144
303 S 5th St   WEBSITE   www.rwamysterysuspense.org/
North Wales PA 19454-3001 USA   newslt.htm
                     EMAIL   pburns@voicenet.com

   ௸ Newsletter of the **Romance Writers of America Mystery & Suspense Chapter**. Articles on writing and mystery-suspense related research, member & market news, and new releases.

KRING AFTONLAMPANS SKEN

Jan Reimer, Editor
Nordmannavägen 30
224 75 Lund SWEDEN

   ௸ Irregular magazine republishing older, public-domain stories of mystery, horror, and supernatural.

Marvin Lachman

5 Oriente Ct
Santa Fe NM 87505 USA

EMAIL   lachman2@earthlink.net

☏ Reviews for *Mystery Readers Journal* and many other mystery publications. Welcomes review copies of short story anthologies and collections in particular.

Läst & Hört I Hängmattan

Iwan Hedman-Morelius, Editor
Calle Acacia, 8
Pinar de Campoverde
El Pilar de la Horadada
03190 Alicante SPAIN

PHONE   +34 60 96 162 11
EMAIL   morelius@terra.es
EMAIL   morelius@vianwe.com

☏ "Read & Listened in the Hammock." Reviews, articles, interviews. Swedish-language, international scope. Monthly (except Jul–Aug) since 1997.

Library Journal

submissions:
360 Park Ave S
New York NY 10010 USA
subscriptions:
PO Box 16178
North Hollywood CA 91615-6178
   USA

PHONE   1-646-746-6819
FAX   1-646-746-6734
SUBSCRIBE   1-800-588-1030
EMAIL   ljquery@reedbusiness.com
WEBSITE   libraryjournal.reviewsnews.com

☏ Reviews 6000 books/year "to assess the value of a book for the library collection." 20 issues/year. Also reviews audiobooks, CDs, ebooks, POD, and video. Detailed submission guidelines at website.

Richard Lipez

161 Otis Rd
Otis MA 01253-9717 USA

PHONE   1-413-243-0046
FAX   1-413-243-0332
EMAIL   josephw8@prodigy.net

☏ Reviews for *Washington Post Book World.*

Dick Lochte

PO Box 5413
Santa Monica CA 90409-5413 USA

FAX   1-310-396-4488
EMAIL   dlochte@attbi.com

☏ Reviews mysteries for the *Los Angeles Times.* Reviews audio mysteries for *Mystery Scene.*

Jonathan Lowe

PO Box 26073
Tucson AZ 85726-6073 USA

EMAIL   JonFLowe@earthlink.net

☏ Reviews audiobooks for AudiobooksToday.com, *Land Line* trucking magazine, and Cracker Barrel Country Stores at CrackerBarrel.com.

☞ M.A.A.D.: MUTUAL ADMIRATION FROM THE ASYLUM DEPARTMENT

EMAIL	murraymade@aol.com
WEBSITE	www.maadwomen.com

✒ Quarterly newsletter from authors Jaqueline Girdner (aka Claire Daniels) and Lynne Murray. Send email with your postal address to receive. Free.

MAGICAL MYSTERY TOUR

Sue Feder
3 Goucher Woods Ct
Towson MD 21286-5658 USA

PHONE	1-410-847-9737
FAX	1-410-847-9303
WEBSITE	mywebpages.comcast.net/ monkshould/
EMAIL	monkshould@comcast.net

☎ Close to one thousand mystery reviews online. Monthly print edition available for bookstores.

MAGGIE MASON

PO Box 15804
San Diego CA 92175-5804 USA

PHONE	1-619-287-2299
EMAIL	maggiemary@yahoo.com

☎ Reviews mysteries for *Deadly Pleasures*.

MIDNIGHT LOUIE'S SCRATCHING POST-INTELLIGENCER

Carole Nelson Douglas
PO Box 331555
Fort Worth TX 76163-1555 USA

PHONE	1-817-292-6208
EMAIL	cdouglas@catwriter.com
WEBSITE	www.catwriter.com

✒ All the news about the mysteries of Midnight Louie that is "fit to be typed." ML Adopt-a-Cat tours & merchandise, cat causes, reader mail. Twice yearly. Fall issue includes Irene Adler's Postmodern Victorian Gazette covering this relaunched historical suspense series.

MIDWEST BOOK REVIEW

Jim Cox, Editor-in-Chief
278 Orchard Dr
Oregon WI 53575 USA

PHONE	1-608-835-7937
EMAIL	mbr@execpc.com
WEBSITE	www.execpc.com/~mbr/ bookwatch/

☎ Publishes 5 monthly library newsletters distributed in California, Wisconsin, & the upper Midwest; also available at website. Est. 1976. See website for submission guidelines.

☞ MINNESOTA CRIME WAVE

1239 Edmund Ave
Saint Paul MN 55104 USA

EMAIL	minnesotacrimewave@yahoo.com
WEBSITE	www.MinnesotaCrimeWave.org

✒ Four Minnesota authors—Carl Brookins, Ellen Hart, William Kent Krueger, and Deborah Woodworth—conspire to promote their books through this newsletter three times a year.

☞ MPM

Kristen Whitbread, Editor   WEBSITE   www.mpmbooks.com
PO Box 180
Libertytown MD 21762-0180 USA

☆ A bulletin on "the doings and undoings" of Barbara Michaels/ Elizabeth Peters/ Barbara Mertz. Available by postal mail and download from website.

Murder Most Cozy

Jan Dean   PHONE   1-228-255-6923
8340 Makiki Dr   EMAIL   jandean@bellsouth.net
Diamondhead MS 39525 USA

❧ A bimonthly subscription newsletter on cozy mysteries and their American & British authors. Interviews, profiles, upcoming releases, crimeless cozies. Maintains an archive.

Mysterical-E

Denise Baton, Editor-in-Chief   EMAIL   frogmountain@earthlink.net
    WEBSITE   welcome.to/mysterical-e/

⌀ An e-zine "run by mystery lovers for mystery lovers." Open to cross-genre, supernatural, and fantastical. Short stories and short films. Contests. Interviews and reviews. Submission guidelines at website.

Mysterious Women

Sara Berger, Editor   EMAIL   sara.berger@the-spa.com
PO Box 2122   WEBSITE   www.sarapublishing.com
Amherst MA 01004-2122 USA

❧ Quarterly newsletter on mystery series written by women. Reviews, interviews, bookstore information, articles. New editor. Est. 1995.

Mystery & Detective Monthly

Cap'n Bob Napier, Editor & Publisher   PHONE   1-253-756-7998
5601 N 40th St   EMAIL   capnbob7@msn.com
Tacoma WA 98407-2701 USA

❧ MDM, "The Magazine of Great Letterature." Letters, news, new releases, chat. Publisher plans to discontinue after 200th issue, Sept. 2003.

The Mystery Magazine

Mr. Fu-Er Lin, Publisher   PHONE   +886 2 2594 6699
32, 1/F, Lane 84   FAX   +886 2 2596 2288
Hsinshen North Road, Section 3
Taipei TAIWAN

❧ Est. 1984. Monthly. Chinese language.

MYSTERY NEWS

Black Raven Press	FAX	1-847-541-4749
105 E Townline Rd #152	EMAIL	caldrich@blackravenpress.com
Vernon Hills IL 60061-1424 USA	WEBSITE	www.blackravenpress.com

֍ Est. 1979. Each bimonthly issue includes 60–70 reviews, 3–6 illuminating interviews, articles & columns, plus dozens of previews and a convention calendar. Newspaper format.

MYSTERY READERS JOURNAL

Janet A Rudolph, Editor	EMAIL	whodunit@murderonthemenu.com
PO Box 8116	WEBSITE	www.mysteryreaders.org
Berkeley CA 94707-8116 USA		

֍ MRJ. Quarterly journal of **Mystery Readers International**. Each issue focuses on mysteries of a specific theme—regional, gardens, sports, etc. Lots of news and reviews.

THE MYSTERY REVIEW

Barbara Davey, Editor	PHONE	1-613-475-4440
US:	FAX	1-613-475-3400
PO Box 488	EMAIL	mystrev@reach.net
Wellesley Island NY 13640-0488 USA	WEBSITE	www.TheMysteryReview.com
Canadian:		
PO Box 233		
Colborne ON K0K 1S0 CANADA		

֍ A Publication for Mystery & Suspense Readers. Quarterly. Articles, reviews, interviews; no fiction.

MYSTERY SCENE

Kate Stine, Editor-in-Chief	PHONE	1-212-765-7124
331 W 57th St, Ste 148	FAX	1-212-765-1381
New York NY 10019-3101 USA	EMAIL	KateStine@mysteryscenemag.com
	WEBSITE	www.MysterySceneMag.com

֍ Est. 1985. Lively, expert mystery coverage with an emphasis on the creative life. Packed with articles by well-known authors; criticism; interviews; corporate publishing and small press news; and an extensive array of book, audio, theater, film and tv reviews.

MYSTERYNET: THE ONLINE MYSTERY NETWORK

Steve Schaffer	PHONE	1-415-284-5410
PO Box 470187	FAX	1-415-284-5401
San Francisco CA 94147 USA	EMAIL	editor@mysterynet.com
	WEBSITE	www.mysterynet.com

⌖ Entertainment, discussion, information, and resources for mystery fans. Original online fiction, weekly cases to solve, a history of the mystery, and lots more. Home to the official websites for Agatha Christie, Nancy Drew, and "Clue Chronicles."

THE NEW YORK TIMES BOOK REVIEW

Charles McGraff, Editor
229 W 43rd St
New York NY 10036-3959 USA

PHONE	1-212-556-1234
FAX	1-212-556-7088
TOLLFREE	1-800-631-2580
WEBSITE	www.nytimes.com/pages/books/review/

☏ Sunday supplement also available by separate subscription. Distributed nationally.

NOT SO MODERN TIMES

Sharan Newman
18645 SW Farmington Rd #255
Aloha OR 97007-7699 USA

FAX	1-503-259-9790
EMAIL	sharan@hevanet.com
WEBSITE	www.hevanet.com/sharan/Levendeur.html

∅ Irregular newsletter from the author of the Catherine Levendeur series. Free. Email or mail her to join mailing list.

NUNS, MOTHERS, AND OTHERS

Lora Roberts, Editor
PO Box 957
Palo Alto CA 94302-0957 USA

EMAIL	jonnie@jonniejacobs.com
WEBSITE	www.nmomysteries.com

∅ Newsletter from and about Lee Harris (nuns), Jonnie Jacobs & Valerie Wolzien (mothers), and Lora Roberts (others). Send postal address to subscribe.

PAPERBACK PARADE

Gary Lovisi, Editor
PO Box 209
Brooklyn NY 11228-0209 USA

PHONE	1-718-646-6126
EMAIL	orders@gryphonbooks.com
WEBSITE	www.gryphonbooks.com

👓 The Magazine for Paperback Readers and Collectors. Est. 1986. Bimonthly. Interviews, news, letters, articles. Cover reproductions of scarce collectibles.

PARTNERS IN CRIME NEWSLETTER

Susan Wittig Albert & Bill Albert
PO Box 1616
Bertram TX 78605-0619 USA

PHONE	1-512-355-2799
EMAIL	china@mail.tstar.net
WEBSITE	www.mysterypartners.com

∅ Newsletter (about 2/yr) from Susan Wittig Albert, author of the China Bayles series, and Bill Albert, who also write together as Robin Paige. Monthly electronic newsletter available at website.

PLOTS WITH GUNS

Anthony Neil Smith, Editor

EMAIL	ansmith@plotswithguns.com
WEBSITE	www.PlotsWithGuns.com

∅ Online-only crime journal of fiction, poetry, and creative nonfiction—as long as it's got a gun in it. New issues bimonthly. Fiction, poetry, and essays in the hardboiled/noir tradition, but not period pastiches.

PUBLISHERS WEEKLY

Peter Cannon, Assoc. Review Ed.	PHONE	1-212-463-6758
360 Park Ave S	FAX	1-212-463-6631
New York NY 10010 USA	WEBSITE	publishersweekly.reviewsnews.com

☞ Weekly trade journal of publishing includes over 130 reviews in every issue. Submit galleys 3 months before publication. Does not review self-published. Detailed guidelines at website.

LEV RAPHAEL

4695 Chippewa Dr	PHONE	1-517-349-5243
Okemos MI 48864-2059 USA	FAX	1-517-349-8873
	EMAIL	levraphael@attbi.com

☞ Mysteries columnist and reviewer for *Detroit Free Press;* book critic for NPR's *Todd Mundt Show;* reviewer for *Jerusalem Report, Washington Post,* and *Forward;* and all-around bon vivant.

THE REASONING NOVEL

Ey-shem Cheng, Publisher	PHONE	+852 2353 5856
Forward Book Company	FAX	+852 2329 6586
PO Box 89311		
Kowloon City HONG KONG		

∞ Chinese language. Est. 1996. Bimonthly.

RED HERRINGS

Peter Guttridge, Editor
Bank Cottage, Streat Lane
Streat, Hassocks, W. Sussex BN6 8RT
  ENGLAND
  ∞ Monthly journal for members of **The Crime Writers' Association.**

REFLECTIONS IN A PRIVATE EYE

Thomas J Sweeney, Editor	EMAIL	pwanewsletter@cs.com
1176 Woodbury Ave		
Portsmouth NH 03801-3248 USA		

  ∞ Newsletter of the **Private Eye Writers of America.**

REICHENBACH JOURNAL

Michael A Meer	PHONE	+41 31 991 63 01
Morgenstrasse 70		
3018 Bern SWITZERLAND		

  § Journal of the **Reichenbach Irregulars.**

RIPLEY'S GARDEN PLOTS

Ann Ripley	PHONE	1-303-823-9329
PO Box 2527	FAX	1-303-823-9689
Lyons CO 80540-2527 USA	EMAIL	annripley@compuserve.com

  ℓ Newsletter from the author of a series of gardening mysteries featuring Louise Eldridge, TV garden show hostess and foreign service wife.

Romantic Times BOOKclub Magazine

Laurie Davie, Mystery Editor
55 Bergen St
Brooklyn NY 11201-6336 USA

PHONE 1-718-237-1097
FAX 1-718-624-2526
SUBSCRIBE 1-800-989-8816
EMAIL LDavie@romantictimes.com
WEBSITE www.romantictimes.com

੬੭ Formerly *Romantic Times*. RT BOOKclub has an extensive mystery review section, which includes many mainstream mysteries as well as those with a romantic suspense element. Gives **RT Reviewers' Choice Awards.**

Ruumiin kulttuuri

Risto Raitio, Editor
PL 6
00551 Helsinki FINLAND

PHONE +358 9 0205 811 288
FAX +358 9 0205 811 288
EMAIL risto.raitio@dekkariseura.fi
WEBSITE www.dekkariseura.fi

੬੭ Quarterly magazine of **Suomen dekkariseura**, the Finnish Whodunit Society. Website has English summary of current issue.

Scarlet Street

Richard Valley, Editor
PO Box 604
Glen Rock NJ 07452-0604 USA

PHONE 1-201-445-0034
FAX 1-201-445-1496
EMAIL reditor@aol.com
WEBSITE ScarletStreet.com

੬੭ Bimonthly glossy. More emphasis on horror, but includes mystery as well. Classic & contemporary movies, TV, & books. Illustrated.

Tom & Enid Schantz

PO Box 4119
Boulder CO 80306-4119 USA

PHONE 1-303-443-5757
FAX 1-303-443-4010
EMAIL Tomenid@attbi.com

☞ Mystery columnists for the *Denver Post.*

Scuttlebutt from the Spermaceti Press

Peter E. Blau, Editor & Publisher
3900 Tunlaw Rd NW #119
Washington DC 20007-4830 USA

EMAIL pblau@dgsys.com
WEBSITE members.cox.net/sherlock1/
scuttle.htm

§ Six or more pages a month of "whatever gossip the editor finds appropriate; much of it quite trivial, but most of it Sherlockian or Doylean."

Sherlock Holmes, The Detective Magazine

David Stuart Davies, BSI, Editor
PO Box 100
Chichester, West Sussex PO18 8HD
ENGLAND

PHONE +44 1243 576444
FAX +44 1243 576456
EMAIL admin@pmh.uk.com
WEBSITE www.pmh.uk.com/sherlock/
sherlock.htm

§ News and articles about Sherlock Holmes, classic and modern detective fiction. Published 6 times yearly. Gives the **Sherlock Awards.** Free sample copy available.

THE SHERLOCKIAN TIMES FROM CLASSIC SPECIALTIES

Carolyn & Joel Senter	PHONE	1-513-281-4757
PO Box 19058	FAX	1-513-281-5797
Cincinnati OH 45219-0058 USA	EMAIL	sherlock@sherlock-holmes.com
	WEBSITE	www.sherlock-holmes.com

§ An informative annual catalog/newsletter/journal with Sherlockian news as well as books, monographs, and accessories. Now supplemented by an email newsletter.

SHOTS

Mike Stotter, Editor	PHONE	+44 181 504 9702
189 Snakes Lane East	EMAIL	mike_stotter@yahoo.co.uk
Woodford Green, Essex IG8 7JH	WEBSITE	www.shotsmag.co.uk
ENGLAND		

⌀ An on-line ezine featuring fiction, nonfiction, interviews, reviews, writing tips and much more. Normally updated every 9 weeks. Members who sign up for free newsletter get to see exclusive material. Submission guidelines at website.

BRUCE E SOUTHWORTH REVIEWS

1621 Lafond Ave	PHONE	1-651-644-1677
Saint Paul MN 55104-2212 USA	FAX	1-651-646-8199
	EMAIL	bruces1@mindspring.com

☞ Monthly mystery review column for *Minneapolis Star Tribune*. Other freelance work has included *St Paul Pioneer Press*, *BookPage*, *Drood Review* and others. Co-producer of *Speaking of Mysteries*, a half hour regional cable television program featuring interviews with mystery authors.

☞ STEVEN STEINBOCK

10 Hickory Ln	EMAIL	stevo1@maine.rr.com
Yarmouth ME 04096-8340 USA		

☞ Regularly reviews mystery and suspense audiobooks for *AudioFile* magazine and *Mystery Readers Journal*.

THE STRAND MAGAZINE

Andrew F Gulli, Managing Editor	PHONE	1-248-788-5948
Jackie Acampora, Book Review Editor	FAX	1-248-874-1046
PO Box 1418	TOLLFREE	1-800-300-6652
Birmingham MI 48012-1418 USA	EMAIL	strandmag@worldnet.att.net
	WEBSITE	www.strandmag.com
	WEBSITE	www.shopmysteries.com

☜ Est. 1999, well-designed glossy quarterly revives the tradition of the famous old magazine with short mystery fiction, Sherlockiana, articles, reviews. Submission guidelines at website. UK toll-free 0800 961 280.

☞ SHINJI TAKARAMURA

2-5-2, Utsukushigaoka #402   EMAIL   QWT01070@nifty.ne.jp
Aoba-ku, Yokohama 225-0002 JAPAN

☞ Writes a column for *Hayakawa's Mystery Magazine* that introduces English language mystery writers not in translation. Many Japanese read books in English, either for pleasure or to improve their English skills. Takaramura-san's column can also bring a writer to the attention of Japanese publishers.

TANGLED WEB (MAGAZINE)

Andrew Osmond
69 Holm Oak Park
Watford, Herts. WD1 8TH ENGLAND

☞ Est. 1996. Promotes the re-reading of some of the more obscure detective fiction writers of the past. Articles on book collecting, author profiles, short stories, contemporary reviews, etc. (Not related to the Tangled Web website.)

TANGLED WEB (WEBSITE)

Liz & Ralph Lees   EMAIL   books@twbooks.co.uk
36 Jebb Lane, Haigh   EMAIL   hickafric@freenet.co.uk
Barnsley, S Yorkshire S75 4BV   WEBSITE   www.twbooks.co.uk
    ENGLAND

☞ UK's leading crime & mystery fiction web site. News, reviews, bibs, awards, author pages, links. Online sales of new and used books, first editions.

LA TÊTE EN NOIR

Jean-Paul Guéry
3 rue Lenepveu
49100 Angers FRANCE

☞ A bimonthly (6/yr) newsletter in French. News and reviews. Occasional supplement, *La Tête en Rose,* for romantic suspense. Send one international reply coupon for sample copy.

☞ THE3RDEGREE.COM

Anthony Dauer, Editor   EMAIL   editor@the3rdegree.com
                              WEBSITE   www.the3rdegree.com

☞ Formerly judas_ezine, The3rdegree.com is a quarterly online publication dedicated to hard-boiled and noir crime fiction. Guidelines for submission are available on the web site.

THE THIRD DEGREE

Suzanne Proulx, Editor   EMAIL   ttd-editor@mysterywriters.org
1230 S Harrison St
Denver CO 80210 USA

☞ Newsletter of the **Mystery Writers of America**, published 10 times a year. Please submit items for newsletter one month in advance, by e-mail only. Preferred format is Word document attachment.

ROBIN WINKS

Boston Globe	PHONE	1-203-432-7599
1785 Middletown Ave	FAX	1-203-484-1177
Northford CT 06472 USA		

☏ Reviews for *Boston Globe*.

WOMAN'S WORLD

Jimmy Meiss, Fiction Dept
270 Sylvan Ave
Englewood Cliffs NJ 07632 USA

👓 Has a "mini-mystery" in every issue.

SUSANNA YAGER

Dunsmore	FAX	+44 20 8422 1998
South Hill Ave	EMAIL	c4tv2@online.rednet.co.uk
Harrow, Middlesex HA1 3PB		
ENGLAND		

☏ Reviews for the *Sunday Telegraph,* London.

Independent Publishers

A.S.A.P. PUBLISHING

Jim & Mary Seels	PHONE	1-949-455-1319
23852 Via Navarra	FAX	1-949-455-1359
Mission Viejo CA 92691-3640 USA	EMAIL	asap-publishing@cox.net

📖 Does several collectible limited editions a year of mystery and dark suspense/horror. Occasional newsletter.

ADDICUS BOOKS

Rod Colvin	PHONE	1-402-330-7493
PO Box 45327	FAX	1-402-330-1707
Omaha NE 68145-0327 USA	ORDERS	1-800-352-2873
	EMAIL	info@addicusbooks.com
	WEBSITE	www.addicusbooks.com

📖 Non-fiction only. True crime books that read like fiction. Seeking submissions; writers guidelines available at website or by mail.

ALLEN A KNOLL PUBLISHERS

200 W Victoria St	PHONE	1-805-564-3377
Santa Barbara CA 93101-3627 USA	FAX	1-805-966-6657
	TOLLFREE	1-800-777-7623
	EMAIL	bookinfo@knollpublishers.com
	WEBSITE	www.knollpublishers.com

📖 Books for intelligent people who read for fun. Featuring mystery and suspense fiction, including Bomber Hanson mysteries and Gil Yates P. I. novels. Sorry, no submissions, please.

ALLISON & BUSBY, LTD

David Shelley	PHONE	+44 20 7738 7888
Suite 111, Bon Marche Centre	FAX	+44 20 7733 4244
241-251 Ferndale Rd	MAIL	all@allisonandbusby.com
Brixton, London SW9 8BJ	WEBSITE	www.allisonandbusby.com
ENGLAND		

📖 This mid-size British publisher features critically acclaimed writers. Crime fiction novels and omnibus reprints can be ordered online. Submission guidelines at website.

ARGUMENT VERLAG ARIADNE KRIMI

Eppendorfer Weg 95a	PHONE	+49 40 4018 000
20259 Hamburg GERMANY	FAX	+49 40 4018 0020
	EMAIL	verlag@argument.de
	WEBSITE	www.argument.de

📖 Publishes crime novels by women writers, including works originally written in German and German translations of UK and US writers.

AVOCET PRESS

Cynthia Webb
19 Paul Ct
Pearl River NY 10965-1539 USA

PHONE	1-845-620-0986
FAX	1-845-735-6807
TOLLFREE	1-877-4-AVOCET
EMAIL	books@avocetpress.com
WEBSITE	www.avocetpress.com

📖 Publishes mysteries under Memento Mori imprint. Looking for submissions with an unusual point of view.

☞ BARCLAY BOOKS

6161 51st St S
St Petersburg FL 33715 USA

PHONE	1-727-867-0518
FAX	1-727-866-9673
EMAIL	Becki@barclaybooks.com
WEBSITE	www.barclaybooks.com

📖 Publisher of action/adventure, dark suspense, drama, fantasy, horror, mystery, science fiction, supernatural thrillers, and suspense fiction.

BASKERVILLE BOOKS

Box 19
3561 Sheppard Ave East
Toronto ON M1T 3K8 CANADA

EMAIL	info@baskervillebooks.com
WEBSITE	www.baskervillebooks.com

📖 Plans to publish three books a year, mostly fiction, in the areas of mystery, dark fantasy, gay lit and gay erotica. Not open to submissions at this time.

THE BATTERED SILICON DISPATCH BOX

George A Vanderburgh, Publisher
PO Box 204
Shelburne ON L0N 1S0 CANADA
US:
PO Box 122
Sauk City WI 53583-0122 USA

FAX	1-519-925-3482
EMAIL	gav@bmts.com

§ Sherlockian and similar vintage detective stories and commentary. Extensive catalog, available by mail.

☞ BLEAK HOUSE BOOKS

Diversity Incorporated
PO Box 8573
Madison WI 53708 USA

EMAIL	bleakhouse@diversityincorporated.com
WEBSITE	www.diversityincorporated.com

📖 Imprint of Diversity Inc for their crime, suspense, and horror fiction. Submission guidelines at website.

BOOK HUNTER PRESS

David S & Susan Siegel	PHONE	1-914-245-6608
PO Box 193	FAX	1-914-245-2630
Yorktown Heights NY 10598-0193	EMAIL	bookhunterpress@earthlink.net
USA	WEBSITE	bookhunterpress.com

📖 Publishers of *The Used Book Lover's Guides,* a series of seven regional guides to over 8,000 used, out-of-print and antiquarian book dealers in the United States and Canada.

BOSON BOOKS

C&M Online Media	PHONE	1-919-233-8164
3905 Meadow Field Ln	FAX	1-919-233-8578
Raleigh NC 27606-4470 USA	EMAIL	cm@cmonline.com
	WEBSITE	www.bosonbooks.com

⌀ Electronic publisher has novels for downloading or on disk. Read free stories to sample an author, then buy a book. No unsolicited submissions, please.

BUFFALO MEDICINE BOOKS

Ernie Bulow	PHONE	1-505-722-2904
PO Box 1762	FAX	1-505-722-3465
Gallup NM 87305-1762 USA	EMAIL	ernie@buffalomedicine.com
	WEBSITE	www.buffalomedicine.com

📖 Limited editions of Tony Hillerman and other Southwestern authors, with original illustrations by Navajo artist Ernest Franklin. Posters of the works of Tony Hillerman.

CALABASH PRESS

Christopher & Barbara Roden	PHONE	1-250-453-2045
PO Box 1360	FAX	1-250-453-2075
Ashcroft BC V0K 1A0 CANADA	WEBSITE	www.ash-tree.bc.ca/calabash.html
	EMAIL	ashtree@ash-tree.bc.ca

§ Specializes in Sherlockiana and the work of Sir Arthur Conan Doyle. Catalog available.

☞ CAPRA PRESS

Robert Bason, Publisher	FAX	1-805-892-2722
815 De La Vina St	PHONE	1-805-892-2721
Santa Barbara CA 93101 USA	WEBSITE	www.caprapress.com

📖 Mystery authors Richard Barre and Dennis Lynds (aka Michael Collins) are both on the advisory board of this fine small press, founded in 1969.

CC PUBLISHING

John C & Cathie Celestri	EMAIL	ccpub@worldnet.att.net
PO Box 542	WEBSITE	www.mysterypublishers.com/CC/
Loveland OH 45140-0542 USA		

📖 Character-driven mysteries and historical crime fiction. Not accepting submissions.

COFFEE CUP PRESS

Victoria Esposito-Shea & Jamey
  Dumas, Editors
33 State St
Canton NY 13617 USA

EMAIL   info@handheldcrime.com
WEBSITE   www.handheldcrime.com/ebooks/
EMAIL   victoria@handheldcrime.com

✒ "With murder and mayhem for the price of a mocha." New e-publishing imprint of HandHeldCrime. Books available for hand-held PDAs, or in PDF format. Purchase and download online.

CREATIVE ARTS BOOK COMPANY

Richard Silver, Senior Editor
833 Bancroft Way
Berkeley CA 94710-2287 USA

PHONE   1-510-848-4777
FAX   1-510-848-4844
TOLLFREE   1-800-848-7789
EMAIL   staff@creativeartsbooks.com
WEBSITE   www.creativeartsbooks.com

📖 Originators of the Black Lizard imprint, still publishing mysteries. Submission guidelines at the website.

CRIPPEN & LANDRU PUBLISHERS

Douglas Greene
PO Box 9315
Norfolk VA 23505-0315 USA

PHONE/FAX   1-757-622-6656
TOLLFREE   1-877-622-6656
EMAIL   CrippenL@pilot.infi.net
WEBSITE   www.crippenlandru.com

📖 Specializing in collections of mystery short stories by a single author. Issues special limited editions for collectors, as well as trade editions.

CRUM CREEK PRESS/ DROOD REVIEW BOOKS

Jim Huang, Editor
484 E Carmel Dr #378
Carmel IN 46032-2812 USA

FAX   1-317-705-1402
EMAIL   info@droodreview.com
WEBSITE   www.droodreview.com/crumcreek/crumcreek.htm

📖 Books for the mystery fiction fan, including reviews, essays, and entertainment.

DEADLY ALIBI PRESS, LTD

Margo Power
PO Box 5947
Vancouver WA 98668-5947 USA

PHONE   1-360-695-9004
FAX   1-360-693-3354
TOLLFREE   1-800-695-9003
WEBSITE   www.deadlyalibipress.com
EMAIL   powermargo@attbi.com

📖 Mystery and suspense fiction and related nonfiction. Guidelines and ordering information at website.

DEADLY SERIOUS PRESS

Kate Derie, Publisher	PHONE	1-520-742-6946
6702 N Casas Adobes Dr	FAX	1-520-742-4179
Tucson AZ 85704-6124 USA	EMAIL	info@deadlyserious.com
	WEBSITE	www.deadlyserious.com

📖 Non-fiction only. Publishes genre-related reference, critical, and biographical. Book proposals welcome. Est. 1994.

DENNIS MCMILLAN PUBLICATIONS

4460 N Hacienda del Sol (Guest House)	PHONE	1-520-529-6636
	EMAIL	dennismcmillan@aol.com
Tucson AZ 85718 USA	WEBSITE	www.dennismcmillan.com

📖 Collectible limited editions of hardboiled mysteries, modern fiction, graphic short stories, "outré literature."

DIOMO BOOKS

Renee Bailey, Editor	PHONE/FAX	1-417-338-0073
427 Austin Place	EMAIL	info@diomobooks.com
Branson West MO 65737 USA	WEBSITE	www.diomobooks.com

📖 Award-winning mystery fiction and specialty non-fiction.

THE DO-NOT PRESS

Jim Driver, Publisher	PHONE	+44 20 8698 7813
16 The Woodlands	FAX	+44 20 8698 7834
London SE13 6TY ENGLAND	EMAIL	jim@thedonotpress.co.uk
	WEBSITE	www.thedonotpress.co.uk

📖 Features crime and mystery fiction that is "modern, thought-provoking and on the cutting-edge of the genre." Submission guidelines (discouraging but amusing) at the website. Est. 1994.

ENVIROCRIME PUBLISHERS

c/o CAE Consultants	PHONE	1-914-963-3695
41 Travers Ave	FAX	1-914-376-5011
Yonkers NY 10705-1648 USA	EMAIL	envirocrime@usa.com
	WEBSITE	www.envirocrime.com

📖 Publishers of the EnviroCrime mystery series. Free monthly email newsletter that summarizes environmental crimes around the world.

FIVE STAR PRESS

Gale	TOLLFREE	1-800-877-GALE
PO Box 9187	FAX ORDERS	1-800-414-5043
Farmington Hills MI 48333-9187	EMAIL	galeord@gale.com
USA	WEBSITE	www.galegroup.com/fivestar/

📖 Established publisher now featuring a mystery line, 6–8 titles every quarter, available through normal distribution channels or by subscription. Individual books may be ordered at the website or by phone or mail.

FULL MOON PUBLISHING

Dee Holder, Senior Editor	ORDERS	1-800-247-6553
PO Box 408	EMAIL	fulmoonpub@aol.com
Schererville IN 46375-0408 USA	WEBSITE	www.fullmoonpub.com

📖 All titles released on the date of a full moon. Welcomes manuscripts that cross mystery with a dose of the unknown—paranormal, fantasy, horror. Est. 1998.

GOLDEN EAGLE PRESS

Mary Lou Romagno, Publisher	PHONE	1-661-327-4290
PO Box 80187	FAX	1-661-393-6157
Bakersfield CA 93380-0187 USA	EMAIL	mapp@goldeneaglepress.com
	WEBSITE	www.goldeneaglepress.com

📖 "Small woman-owned press strives to publish those authors who have something unique to say, whether it be autobiography, fiction, history or self improvement." Submissions welcome.

☞ GRYPHON BOOKS

Gary Lovisi, Publisher	PHONE	1-718-646-6126
PO Box 209	EMAIL	orders@gryphonbooks.com
Brooklyn NY 11228-0209 USA	WEBSITE	www.gryphonbooks.com

📖 Publishers of new fiction, reference, Sherlockian, and facsimile editions of classic pulp.

HANNACROIX CREEK BOOKS, INC

1127 High Ridge Rd #110	PHONE	1-203-321-8674
Stamford CT 06905-1203 USA	EMAIL	hannacroix@aol.com
	WEBSITE	www.hannacroix.com

📖 Est. 1996. "Committed to publishing excellent books... that inspire, entertain, or educate." Titles have been translated into several foreign languages. Not accepting unsolicited manuscripts.

HARD SHELL WORD FACTORY

Mary Wolf, Publisher & Editor-in-Chief	EMAIL	books@hardshell.com
PO Box 161	WEBSITE	www.hardshell.com
Amherst Junction WI 54407-0161 USA		

⊘ 📖 Mystery, suspense and other genres, published in trade paperback and downloadable e-books in many formats. Submissions only by referral or invitation at this time. Watch website during 2003 for submission opening announcments.

HOUSE OF STRATUS

Thirsk Industrial Park	PHONE	+44 1845 527700
York Road	FAX	+44 1845 527711
Thirsk, North Yorkshire YO7 3BX	EMAIL	info@houseofstratus.com
ENGLAND	WEBSITE	www.houseofstratus.com

📖 Publisher of recent and vintage crime fiction, using print-on-demand technology to maintain a lengthy backlist. Est. 1999.

InterContinental Publishing

H G Smittenaar
PO Box 7242
Fairfax Station VA 22039 USA

PHONE 1-703-369-4992
FAX 1-703-670-7825
EMAIL icpub@worldnet.att.net
WEBSITE home.att.net/~icpub/

📖 Publisher of several Dutch authors in English translation, also original American mysteries and children's books.

Intrigue Press

PO Box 102004
1310 S Washington St
Denver CO 80210 USA

PHONE 1-303-777-0539
FAX 1-303-756-8011
TOLLFREE 1-800-996-9783
EMAIL books@intriguepress.com
WEBSITE www.intriguepress.com

📖 Traditional mystery and suspense fiction, and international crime fiction. Also interested in literary mysteries; submission guidelines at website.

Japphire

Amy Falen
6947 Coal Creek Parkway SE #1000
Newcastle WA 98059-3136 USA

PHONE 1-425-430-0007
FAX 1-425-204-8877
EMAIL info@japphire.com
WEBSITE www.japphire.com

📖 Specializes in suspense fiction and "industrial thrillers" that explore situations and dangers affecting everyday life. Sorry, no submissions at present.

Kleworks Publishing Company

Mary Welk
6127 N Ozark Ave
Chicago IL 60631-3844 USA

PHONE 1-773-774-3372
FAX 1-773-467-4496
EMAIL kleworks@aol.com
WEBSITE www.mysterykleworks.com

📖 Featuring solidly plotted cozy mysteries.

Koenisha Publications

Sharolett Koenig
3196 53rd St
Hamilton MI 49419-9626 USA

PHONE/FAX 1-616-751-4100
EMAIL koenisha@macatawa.org
WEBSITE www.koenisha.com

📖 Independent publisher featuring the Jacketed SoftCover™ format. Nonfiction and fiction of all kinds, specializing in mysteries for adults as well as young people. 5-10 books/year. Submission guidelines at website.

Leister Publishing Company

6 Forest Glen
Lake Ariel PA 18436-5401 USA

FAX 1-570-689-0820
TOLLFREE 1-877-813-9612
EMAIL info@LeisterPublishing.com
WEBSITE www.LeisterPublishing.com

📖 Action, mystery, suspense, thrillers.

LOCUS PRESS

William G Contento   PHONE   1-510-339-9198
PO Box 13305   EMAIL   locus@locusmag.com
Oakland CA 94661-0305 USA   WEBSITE   https://amber.site-secure.net/
                                      locusmag/About/CDRomAd.html

▭ Publishes CD-ROM versions of mystery references, including Allen Hubin's *Crime Fiction III,* and Contento's index of mystery short fiction. Secure online ordering (note the prefix on the website address).

MYSTERY VAULT

Laura Roberts, Publisher   PHONE   1-941-349-0838
Stuart M Kaminsky, Editor-in-chief FAX   1-941-925-3145
2621 Mall Dr   WEBSITE   www.mysteryvault.com
Sarasota FL 34231-5939 USA

▭ New publisher of classic, hard to obtain, and new mystery novels, in trade paperback format. Many well-known authors. Books may be ordered at website.

NEW VICTORIA PUBLISHERS

PO Box 27   PHONE/FAX   1-802-649-5297
Norwich VT 05055-0027 USA   TOLLFREE   1-800-326-5297
                              EMAIL   newvic@aol.com
                              WEBSITE   www.NewVictoria.com

▭ Publishers of award-winning mystery series by Sarah Dreher and Jean Marcy, as well as many other authors, since 1976. Featuring books with strong female protagonists.

NO EXIT PRESS

18 Coleswood Road   PHONE   +44 1582-761264
Harpenden, Herts AL5 1EQ   FAX   +44 1582-712244
    ENGLAND   EMAIL   editor@noexit.co.uk
                           WEBSITE   www.noexit.co.uk

▭ Leading independent publisher of crime fiction, including UK editions of US authors. No submissions, please.

PALADIN PRESS

Peder Lund   PHONE   1-303-443-7250
Gunbarrel Tech Center   FAX   1-303-443-8741
7077 Winchester Circle TOLLFREE 1-800-392-2400
Boulder CO 80306 USA   EMAIL   service@paladin-press.com
                        WEBSITE   www.paladin-press.com

▭ Non-fiction only. Publisher and bookseller specializing in combat, law enforcement, and survival topics. "Home of the Action Library." Great information source for the thriller writer.

☛ PENDULUM PRESS

Marilyn Henderson
2700 W 44th St # 412
Minneapolis MN 55410-1946 USA

EMAIL marilyn@pendulumpress.com
WEBSITE www.pendulumpress.com

✐ "Electronic publishers of quality mystery and suspense." Books downloadable in several formats; some also in trade paperback editions. Submission guidelines at website.

PERSEVERANCE PRESS/ JOHN DANIEL & CO.

Meredith Phillips, Editor
John Daniel, Publisher
PO Box 21922
Santa Barbara CA 93121-1922 USA

PHONE 1-805-962-1780
FAX 1-805-962-8835
ORDERS 1-800-662-8351
EMAIL dandd@danielpublishing.com
WEBSITE www.danielpublishing.com/perseverance/

📖 Joint venture bringing out new literary mystery novels with an emphasis on excellent writing, suspenseful plots, and meaningful characters and situations. Looking for established writers who would like to begin a new series or continue an old one with a new publisher.

POISONED PEN PRESS

Robert Rosenwald, President
6962 E 1st Ave #103
Scottsdale AZ 85251-4302 USA

PHONE 1-480-945-3375
FAX 1-480-949-1707
TOLLFREE 1-800-421-3976
EMAIL info@poisonedpenpress.com
WEBSITE www.poisonedpenpress.com

📖 Original mysteries, mystery reference books, and "missing mysteries" (new editions of out-of-print mysteries).

POPULAR PRESS

1930 Monroe St, 3rd Fl
Madison WI 53711-2059 USA

PHONE 1-608-263-0165
FAX 1-608-263-1120
EMAIL rpknutso@wisc.edu
WEBSITE www.wisc.edu/wisconsinpress/popularpress.html

📖 Academic press which offers a number of books studying the relationship between detective fiction and popular culture, as well as critical/biographical studies of mystery fiction writers. Effective July 1, 2002, Popular Press moved to the University of Wisconsin, which will continue to publish new titles and backlist.

PUBLISHAMERICA, INC

PO Box 151
Frederick MD 21705-0151 USA

EMAIL writers@PublishAmerica.com
WEBSITE www.PublishAmerica.com

📖 Specializes in fiction and nonfiction "about/for people who face a major challenge in life and who are determined to overcome...." Includes mystery and suspense novels. Will accept unagented submissions.

PURPLE MOON PRESS

Willetta L Heising	EMAIL	willetta@purplemoonpress.com
3319 Greenfield Rd, #317	WEBSITE	www.purplemoonpress.com
Dearborn MI 48120-1212 USA		

📖 Non-fiction only. Publisher of mystery series reader's guides, including *Detecting Women* and *Detecting Men*, and sponsor of **Mystery Series Week**.

RAINBOW BOOKS, INC

Betsy Lampe, Ed. Dir.	PHONE	1-863-648-4420
PO Box 430	FAX	1-863-647-5951
Highland City FL 33846-0430 USA	EMAIL	RBIbooks@aol.com

📖 Est. 1979. Interested in developing first-time authors with character-driven work who want to actively participate in marketing. Send a SASE for writer guidelines.

RENDEZVOUS PRESS

Sylvia McConnell, Publisher	PHONE	1-416-730-9052
1005-3266 Yonge St	FAX	1-416-226-9975
Toronto ON M4N 3P6 CANADA	EMAIL	transmedia@sympatico.ca
	WEBSITE	www.transmedia95.com

📖 RendezVous Crime series seeks to introduce new voices and features unconventional and very modern plotlines. Canadian submissions only please.

THE RUE MORGUE PRESS

Tom & Enid Schantz	PHONE	1-303-443-5757
PO Box 4119	FAX	1-303-443-4010
Boulder CO 80306-4119 USA	WEBSITE	www.ruemorguepress.com
	EMAIL	Tomenid@attbi.com

📖 Specializes in reprints of classic mysteries. Catalog available entitled *For Old Crimes Sake*.

RUPERT BOOKS

R Dixon Smith & Paulina M Smith	PHONE	+44 1954 781861
58/59 Stonefield	EMAIL	sales@rupert-books.co.uk
Bar Hill	WEBSITE	www.rupert-books.co.uk
Cambridge CB3 8TE ENGLAND		

§ Books and monographs relating to Sherlock Holmes, Arthur Conan Doyle, & Jack the Ripper. No submissions, please.

SALVO PRESS

Scott Schmidt, Publisher	PHONE/FAX	1-541-330-8746
PO Box 9095	EMAIL	salvopress@hotmail.com
Bend OR 97708-9095 USA	WEBSITE	www.salvopress.com

📖 ⌀ Mystery, suspense and thriller novels in trade paper and most eBook formats. "Consider us the micro brew of the industry, hand-crafted novels with a distinct flavor."

SAVAGE PRESS

Michael P Savage, Publisher
PO Box 115
Superior WI 54880-0115 USA

TOLLFREE 1-800-732-3867
EMAIL savpress@spacestar.net
WEBSITE www.savpress.com

📖 Stories of significance regarding the culture, history, geography and spirituality of the Midwest. Publishes 5–10 books a year, including mystery fiction among other fiction and non-fiction.

SAVVY PRESS

473 17th St #6
Brooklyn NY 11215-6226 USA

FAX 1-443-238-0770
EMAIL info@savvypress.com
WEBSITE www.savvypress.com

📖 An independent publisher of fiction, good fiction, and better fiction. No submissions, please.

SCORPION PRESS

Michael Johnson, Proprietor
The Courtyard Barns, Gladestry
Kington, Herefordshire HR5 3NR
ENGLAND

PHONE/FAX +44 1594 370296

📖 Publishers of crime fiction in finely bound, limited editions.

☞ SERPENT'S TAIL

4 Blackstock Mews
London N4 2BT ENGLAND

PHONE +44 171-354-1949
TOLLFREE +44 171-704-6467
EMAIL info@serpentstail.com
WEBSITE www.serpentstail.com

📖 "Committed to publishing extravagant, outlaw voices neglected by the mainstream." Includes new titles and reprints of crime fiction on the hardboiled and noir side. Free shipping anywhere in the world. Currently not accepting submissions but see website.

SILVER DAGGER MYSTERIES

PO Box 1261
Johnson City TN 37605-1261 USA

EMAIL bethw@overmtn.com
WEBSITE silverdaggermysteries.com
WEBSITE www.overmountainpress.com

📖 An imprint of Overmountain Press, specializing in mysteries by a consortium of Southern authors. Submission guidelines at website.

SOHO PRESS

853 Broadway
New York NY 10003-4703 USA

PHONE 1-212-260-1900
FAX 1-212-260-1902
EMAIL bdevendorf@sohopress.com
WEBSITE www.sohopress.com

📖 The Soho Crime series includes hardcover and paperback novels featuring foreign settings and unusual investigators. Catalog, submission guidelines, and ordering information are available at the website or by mail.

ST KITTS PRESS

Elizabeth Whiteker, Senior Editor
PO Box 8173
Wichita KS 67208-8173 USA

PHONE	1-316-685-3201
FAX	1-316-685-6650
TOLLFREE	1-888-705-4887
EMAIL	stkitts@skpub.com
WEBSITE	www.stkittspress.com

📖 Fiction imprint of S-K Publications. Mysteries in a wide range of subgenres.

☛ STEWART MASTERS PUBLISHING, LTD

Roger Stewart, Publisher
27 Hampton Ct
Alameda CA 94502 USA

PHONE/FAX	1-510-864-0966
EMAIL	publisher@stewartmasters.com
WEBSITE	www.stewartmasters.com

📖 Bringing long-unavailable genre classics back into print for fans and collectors.

TIMBERWOLF PRESS

Patrick Seaman, Publisher
202 N Allen Dr Ste A
Allen TX 75013 USA

PHONE	1-972-359-0911
EMAIL	info@timberwolfpress.com
WEBSITE	www.timberwolfpress.com

📖 Books and full-cast audiobooks include mystery and thriller titles. Submission guidelines at website.

TOP PUBLICATIONS, LTD

Lisa Korth, President
mailing:
3100 Independence Pkwy, #311-359
Plano TX 75075-9189 USA

PHONE	1-972-490-9686
FAX	1-972-233-0713
TOLLFREE	1-877-490-9686
EMAIL	info@toppub.com
WEBSITE	www.toppub.com

📖 Publishes general fiction in all genres, including mysteries and legal thrillers. Est. 1998. Submission guidelines at website.

UGLYTOWN

Tom Fassbender & Jim Pascoe
7336 Santa Monica Blvd #683
West Hollywood CA 90046-6616
    USA

PHONE	1-213-484-8334
FAX	1-213-483-5620
EMAIL	mayorsoffice@UglyTown.com
WEBSITE	www.UglyTown.com

📖 Publishers of mysteries and suspense titles, from young adult to hard-boiled fiction. Submission guidelines at website.

WILLOWTREE PRESS

Kathy J Epps
2438 Charlack Ste 1024
Saint Louis MO 63114-4804 USA

PHONE/FAX	1-314-423-3634
EMAIL	info@willowtreepress.com
WEBSITE	www.willowtreepress.com

📖 Specializing in suspense thrillers for the New Age. Est. 1999 to provide quality fiction which portrays Alternative Religions such as Wicca in an accurate and positive light. See website concerning submissions.

Information Resources

☛ AgathaChristie.com: The Official Online Home of Agatha Christie

c/o Agatha Christie Ltd	PHONE	+44 20 7434 1880
40 Shaftesbury Ave	FAX	+44 20 7494 4784
London W1D 7ER England	WEBSITE	www.AgathaChristie.com
	EMAIL	enquiries@agathachristie.co.uk

𝛳 This internet headquarters replaces the Agatha Christie Society. It features a biography, bibliography, calendar of Christie events, and links to electronic newsletters and message forums.

BILIPO: Bibliothèque des Littératures Policières

Catherine Chauchard, Chief Librarian	PHONE	+33 42 34 93 00
48/50 Rue du Cardinal Lemoine	FAX	+33 40 51 81 23
75005 Paris France	EMAIL	100706.1132@compuserve.com

🌱 Public library dedicated to collection, preservation, and study of mystery literature published in French. Annual: *Les Crimes de l'Année: Sélection Critique des Meilleurs Romans Policiers (Crimes of the Year: A Critical Selection of the Best Crime Novels).*

BKA: Bochumer Krimi Archiv

Reinhard Jahn	PHONE	+49 201 765 699
PO Box 10 18 13	EMAIL	100740.3540@compuserve.com
45018 Essen Germany	WEBSITE	homepages.compuserve.de/
		krimijahn/dkp

🌱 Archive of Crime Fiction in German. Awards the **Deutsche Krimi Preis**. BKA originally meant "Bundeskriminalamt," the German equivalent of the FBI.

BoKAS: Bonner Krimi Archiv Sekundärliteratur

Thomas Przybilka	PHONE	+49 228 21 34 10
Buschstrasse 14	PHONE	+49 228 24 21 383
53113 Bonn Germany	FAX	+49 228 24 21 385
	EMAIL	mlbonn@t-online.de

🌱 Est. 1989. Archives references & criticism of the genre, also **Das Syndikat** (German Crime Writers' Association), and German Chapter of Sisters in Crime.

BookWire

	PHONE	1-212-982-7008
	FAX	1-212-337-7050
	WEBSITE	www.bookwire.com

⌀ Everything about the book business, from the publishers of *Publishers Weekly* and *Library Journal.* Author signing schedules, articles, links, forums.

BOSTON COLLEGE: JOHN J BURNS LIBRARY

Robert K O'Neill, Burns Librarian	PHONE	1-617-552-8297
140 Commonwealth Ave	FAX	1-617-552-2465
Chestnut Hill MA 02467-3801 USA	EMAIL	oneillro@bc.edu
	WEBSITE	www.bc.edu/bc_org/aup/ulib/Burns/

🌳 Library & personal papers of Rex Stout, 1886–1975. 2,400 volumes including adaptations for radio & TV. 125 MSS, 21 cubic feet of correspondence. John McAleer Detective Fiction Collection. Kirby Collection of Nick Carter Mysteries.

BOSTON UNIVERSITY: MUGAR MEMORIAL LIBRARY

Dr Howard B Gotlieb, Director	PHONE	1-617-353-3696
Dept of Special Collections	FAX	1-617-353-2838
771 Commonwealth Ave	EMAIL	speccol@bu.edu
Boston MA 02215-1401 USA	WEBSITE	www.bu.edu/speccol/

🌳 Since 1976, home of the **Mystery Writers of America** Library, a collection of books, review copies, and proofs of novels by MWA members. Also many MSS in 20th Century Archives.

BRANDEIS UNIVERSITY LIBRARY

Susan Pyzynski, Special Collections Librarian	PHONE	1-781-736-4686
	FAX	1-781-736-4719
PO Box 549110 Mailstop 045	EMAIL	pyzynski@brandeis.edu
Waltham MA 02454-9110 USA	WEBSITE	www.library.brandeis.edu/SpecialCollections/

🌳 American Literature Dime Novels Collection, cataloged online.

BROWARD COUNTY LIBRARY: BIENES CENTER FOR THE LITERARY ARTS

100 S Andrews Ave Fl 6	PHONE	1-954-357-8667
Fort Lauderdale FL 33301-1830 USA	EMAIL	jfindlay@browardlibrary.org
	WEBSITE	www.co.broward.fl.us/bienes.htm

🌳 This special collections and rare books library contains the archives of Charles Willeford, including manuscripts, letters, and other memorabilia. Holdings listed at website.

UNIVERSITY AT BUFFALO: LOCKWOOD MEMORIAL LIBRARY

Kathleen Quinlivan, Project Asst.	PHONE	1-716-645-2756 EXT 231
Buffalo NY 14260-2200 USA	FAX	1-716-645-3710
	EMAIL	kquin@acsu.buffalo.edu
	WEBSITE	ublib.buffalo.edu/libraries/units/lml/kelley/

🌳 George Kelley Paperback and Pulp Fiction Collection: over 25,000 books & magazines, with detective & mystery the largest category. Also adventure, detective, erotic, fantastic, horror, legal, science fiction, war, western.

CLUELASS.COM

Kate Derie, Editor	PHONE	1-520-742-6946
6702 N Casas Adobes Dr	FAX	1-520-742-4179
Tucson AZ 85704-6124 USA	EMAIL	cluelass@cluelass.com
	WEBSITE	www.cluelass.com

⌀ Webite features list of upcoming books and searchable online version of the *Deadly Directory*, with the addition of award winners, many more online resources & author websites.

COLUMBIA UNIVERSITY: RARE BOOK & MANUSCRIPT LIBRARY

Jean Ashton, Director	PHONE	1-212-854-8480
535 W 114th St	FAX	1-212-854-1365
New York NY 10027-7029 USA	EMAIL	rarebooks@libraries.cul.columbia.edu
	WEBSITE	www.columbia.edu/cu/lweb/indiv/rare/

🌳 Large mystery & detective fiction manuscript collection. Includes papers of Frederick Dannay (one half of Ellery Queen).

CSULB MYSTERY COLLECTION

Leslie Kay Swigart	PHONE	1-562-985-8327
University Library Room 322 West	EMAIL	lswigart@csulb.edu
1250 Bellflower Boulevard	WEBSITE	www.csulb.edu/library/guide/serv/mystery.html
Long Beach CA 90840-1901 USA		

🌳 Mystery, detective, spy and thriller fiction. More than 10,000 copies of more than 4000 titles in the collection. All volumes are fully cataloged in COAST, the library's online catalog, and are available for loan.

DET DANSKE KRIMINALAKADEMIS BIBLIOTEKET

Egebjergvej 210	WEBSITE	www.sherlockiana.net/krimibiblioteket.html
Strandhuse		
4500 Nykøbing Sjælland DENMARK		

🌳 Library of the Danish Academy for Crime Fiction. Danish crime novels, pulps, criticism, EQMM, other collectibles. Holdings catalogued at website. Website in Danish and English.

THE DOROTHY L SAYERS CENTRE

Sue O'Brien, Librarian	PHONE	+44 1376 519625
Witham Library	EMAIL	centre@sayers.org.uk
18 Newland Street		
Witham, Essex CM8 2AQ ENGLAND		

☆ A collection of works by and about Dorothy L Sayers. Open Thursdays 2-5 pm, and at other times by appointment.

UNIVERSITY OF FLORIDA: SMATHERS LIBRARY

Frank Orser, Manuscripts Librarian	PHONE	1-352-392-9075
PO Box 117001	FAX	1-352-846-2746
Gainesville FL 32611-7001 USA	EMAIL	special@mail.uflib.ufl.edu
	WEBSITE	web.uflib.ufl.edu/spec/

🌴 100 linear feet of John D MacDonald MSS, letters, TV and film deals, photos, personal correspondence, and much more. 300 boxes of written materials, with another 53 boxes of photographs.

LE FONDS SIMENON DE L'UNIVERSITÉ DE LIÈGE

Christine Deliège, Conservateur	PHONE	+32 4 366 3022
Château de Colonster	FAX	+32 4 366 5702
Allée des Erables	EMAIL	C.Deliege@ulg.ac.be
4000 Liège BELGIUM	WEBSITE	www.ulg.ac.be/libnet/simenon.htm

🌴 Simenon Foundation provides access to over 7000 works, including editions in French and in translation, manuscripts, dictation cassettes, critical studies, photos, correspondence.

INDIANA UNIVERSITY: LILLY LIBRARY

Breon Mitchell, Director	PHONE	1-812-855-2452
1200 E 7th St	FAX	1-812-855-3143
Bloomington IN 47405-5500 USA	EMAIL	liblilly@indiana.edu
	WEBSITE	www.indiana.edu/~liblilly/

🌴 400,000 books & 6,500,000 manuscripts. Ian Fleming's Bond MSS. & papers of William Anthony Parker White (Anthony Boucher). American & British mysteries & pulps.

UNIVERSITY OF IOWA LIBRARIES

Amy Cooper, Spec. Col. Lib	PHONE	1-319-335-5921
Iowa City IA 52242-1420 USA	FAX	1-319-335-5900
	EMAIL	lib-spec@uiowa.edu
	WEBSITE	www.lib.uiowa.edu/spec-coll/

🌴 Iowa Author's Collection includes mystery authors such as Max Allan Collins and Ed Gorman. Special Collections features the Mabbott-Poe Collection; the "X" collection includes dime novels.

KENT STATE UNIVERSITY LIBRARY

Nancy Birk, Curator & University	PHONE	1-330-672-2770
Archivist	EMAIL	scinfo@lms.kent.edu
Kent OH 44242-0001 USA	WEBSITE	speccoll.library.kent.edu

🌴 1000 volumes including the Raymond Chandler Special Collection, R. Austin Freeman correspondance, Borowitz true crime collection.

LIBRARY OF CONGRESS

Mark Dimunation, Chief	PHONE	1-202-707-5434
Rare Book & Special Collection Division	FAX	1-202-707-4142
	EMAIL	rbsc@loc.gov
101 Independence Ave SE Stop 4376	WEBSITE	lcweb.loc.gov/rr/rarebook/
Washington DC 20540-4376 USA		

🌳 Has 300 pulp fiction magazine series: 15,000 issues from the 1920s to the 1950s. Also 40,000 dime novels.

MERCANTILE LIBRARY OF NEW YORK

Harold Augenbraum, Director	PHONE	1-212-755-6710
17 E 47th St	FAX	1-212-758-1387
New York NY 10017-1980 USA	EMAIL	info@mercantilelibrary.org
	WEBSITE	www.mercantilelibrary.org

🌳 Largest collection of mystery, detective, & crime fiction in US. All 20th century titles circulate to paying members, who can receive books by mail. **Mystery Writers of America** is an Affiliated Organization.

MICHIGAN STATE UNIVERSITY LIBRARIES

Peter Berg, Special Collections	PHONE	1-517-355-3770
100 Library	FAX	1-517-353-5069
East Lansing MI 48824-1048 USA	EMAIL	berg@pilot.msu.edu
	WEBSITE	www.lib.msu.edu/coll/main/spec_col/nye/

🌳 Russel B Nye Popular Culture Collection. 4,000 dime novels, pulps (1920–1950), & detective/mystery novels. Complete runs of *London Mystery Magazine, Ellery Queen's Mystery Magazine, The Armchair Detective.*

THE MYSTERIOUS HOME PAGE

Kate Derie	PHONE	1-520-742-6946
6702 N Casas Adobes Dr	FAX	1-520-742-4179
Tucson AZ 85704-6124 USA	EMAIL	cluelass@cluelass.com
	WEBSITE	www.cluelass.com/MystHome/

⊘ Comprehensive "jump site" with links to everything about mystery on the Web. Regularly updated.

UNIVERSITY OF NORTH CAROLINA, CHAPEL HILL: WILSON LIBRARY

Elizabeth Chenault	PHONE	1-919-962-1143
Rare Book Collection	FAX	1-919-962-4452
CB# 3936 Wilson Library	EMAIL	rbcref@email.unc.edu
Chapel Hill NC 27514-8890 USA	WEBSITE	www.lib.unc.edu/rbc/

🌳 Approx. 12,500 volumes in Barzun-Taylor Mystery-Detective Collection, plus Mary Shore Cameron Collection (Sherlockiana), the Sherlockian Collection of Charles J. Ragland, and American pulp fiction collection.

UNIVERSITY OF NORTH CAROLINA, GREENSBORO: WALTER CLINTON JACKSON LIBRARY

Dr William K Finley, Head
Special Collections & Rare Books
PO Box 26175
Greensboro NC 27402-6175 USA

PHONE 1-336-334-5246
FAX 1-336-334-5399
WEBSITE library.uncg.edu/depts/speccoll/

🌳 Robbie Emily Dunn Collection of American Detective Fiction, "The First 100 Years," 1867–1967, primarily by women, some by men who created women detectives in a series. Also Girls Books in Series Collection.

OBERLIN COLLEGE MAIN LIBRARY

Edward Vermue, Special Collections
4th Floor, Mudd Center
148 W College St
Oberlin OH 44074-1532 USA

PHONE 1-216-775-8285 x264
FAX 1-216-775-8739
EMAIL Ed.Vermue@oberlin.edu
WEBSITE www.oberlin.edu/library/SCP/

🌳 Over 1400 titles of popular fiction from 1906–1985, the Walter F. Tunks Collection of Dime Novels including 2200 titles in 89 series.

OCCIDENTAL COLLEGE: MARY NORTON CLAPP LIBRARY

Michael C Sutherland, Special Collec-
    tions Librarian
1600 Campus Rd
Los Angeles CA 90041-3314 USA

PHONE 1-323-259-2852
FAX 1-323-341-4991
EMAIL bun@oxy.edu
WEBSITE www.oxy.edu/departments/library/
    speccoll/

🌳 Guymon Mystery & Detective Fiction Collection. First editions, manuscripts, film scripts, photographs 1592–1975. 16,000 volumes. British and American.

UNIVERSITY OF PITTSBURGH

Charles E Aston Jr, Special Collec-
    tions
363 Hillman Library
Pittsburgh PA 15260-7303 USA

PHONE 1-412-648-8191
FAX 1-412-648-8192
EMAIL cea@pitt.edu
WEBSITE www.library.pitt.edu/libraries/
    special/special.html

🌳 Mary Roberts Rinehart Collection. 415 volumes, MSS, pictures, & memorabilia. 22 cubic feet of MSS, interviews, & biographical material.

PRINCETON UNIVERSITY LIBRARIES: SPECIAL COLLECTIONS

Margaret Sherry Rich, Reference
    Librarian/Archivist
1 Washington Rd
Princeton NJ 08544-2098 USA

PHONE 1-609-258-3184
FAX 1-609-258-2324
EMAIL msrich@princeton.edu
WEBSITE www.princeton.edu/~rbsc/

🌳 Personal papers of SS Van Dine, Scribner Archives. Collections of James M Cain, Raymond Chandler, A Conan Doyle, Erle Stanley Gardner, Ellery Queen, & Cornell Woolrich.

SHERLOCK HOLMES MUSEET

Egebjergvej 210	PHONE	+45 5932 9238
Strandhuse	EMAIL	sherlockiana@nielsen.mail.dk
4500 Nykøbing Sjælland DENMARK	WEBSITE	www.sherlockiana.net

§ ♣ Sherlock Holmes Museum. One of the largest public collections of Sherlockiana in Europe. Books about Holmes, comics, gramophone records, dolls, stamps, Holmes' violin, etc.

SHERLOCK HOLMES MUSEUM

Bice Musfeld	PHONE	+41 36 714221
Park Hotel du Sauvage	FAX	+41 36 714300
Bahnhofstr. 26	EMAIL	info@sherlockholmes.ch
3860 Meiringen SWITZERLAND	WEBSITE	www.sherlockholmes.ch

§ ♣ Reconstruction of Holmes's living room in the crypt of an English church, now a gallery. Mystery weekends in conjunction with the hotel. Website has lots of Sherlockian info (in German, for now).

SHERLOCKIAN NET

Chris Redmond	PHONE	1-519-886-1207
523 Westfield Drive	EMAIL	credmond@uwaterloo.ca
Waterloo ON N2T 2E1 CANADA	WEBSITE	www.sherlockian.net

§ ⌀ Comprehensive jump site by a serious Sherlockian. Links to illustrations, texts, criticism, absolutely everything about Holmes on the net.

SHERLOCKTRON: AN INTERNET INFORMATION CENTER FOR SHERLOCK HOLMES

Willis G Frick	PHONE	1-949-368-6914
513 Via Presa	FAX	1-949-368-8519
San Clemente CA 92672-9474 USA	EMAIL	sherlock1@cox.net
	WEBSITE	members.cox.net/sherlock1/ Sherlocktron.html

§ ⌀ Comprehensive international database of information on Sherlockian societies, publications, and products.

STADTBIBLIOTHEK BREMEN: KRIMIBIBLIOTHEK

Ulrike Funk	PHONE	+49 421 361 3913
in der Bibliothek Neustadt	FAX	+49 421 361 17292
Friedrich-Ebert-Straße 101/105	EMAIL	funk@edvserv.stabi.uni-bremen.de
28199 Bremen GERMANY	WEBSITE	www.stadtbibliothek-bremen.de/specials/ home.php3?specials=krimi

♣ Public library covering German crime & mystery fiction as well as secondary literature related to crime & mystery. About 4,000 titles at present.

SUNY College at Oneonta: James M Milne Library

Special Collections Librarian   PHONE   1-607-436-2727
Oneonta NY 13820-3414 USA   WEBSITE   www.oneonta.edu/library/scc/
SCC.HTML

🌳 Martha C Chambers Collection of popular fiction of the 19th & early 20th centuries includes American romantic fiction, mysteries, & westerns.

Svenska Deckarbiblioteket

Thomas Böös   PHONE   +46 16 10 12 20
Eskilstuna Stads-Och Länsbibliotek   FAX   +46 16 14 17 56
632 20 Eskilstuna SWEDEN   EMAIL   crimelib@eskilstuna.se
WEBSITE   www.eskilstuna.se/biblioteket/
deckarbiblioteket/

🌳 Swedish Library of Crime Fiction. A research library within the County Library of Södermanland. Open to public on request.

The Thrilling Detective Web Site

Kevin Burton Smith   EMAIL   kvnsmith@thrillingdetective.com
3053 Rancho Vista Blvd Ste H116   WEBSITE   www.thrillingdetective.com
Palmdale CA 93551 USA

⌀ Premier site for fans of private eyes and other tough guys and gals who make trouble their business, with commentary and extensive bibliographies for over 1500 eyes, including appearances in literature, film, TV, radio, and other media. Also fiction, reviews, and a reader's poll.

University of Tulsa: McFarlin Library

Lori N Curtis, Special Collections   PHONE   1-918-631-2496
2933 E 6th St   FAX   1-918-631-5022
Tulsa OK 74104-3123 USA   EMAIL   lori-curtis@utulsa.edu
WEBSITE   www.lib.utulsa.edu/speccoll/

🌳 Early detective fiction, 600 volumes of Sherlockiana, & Graham Greene's collection of translations of his work in many languages. Tage La Cour Collection of Mystery and Science Fiction.

Marion E Wade Center

Christopher Mitchell, Director   PHONE   1-630-752-5908
Wheaton College   FAX   1-630-752-5459
Wheaton IL 60187-5535 USA   EMAIL   wade@wheaton.edu
WEBSITE   www.wheaton.edu/learnres/wade/

🌳 Special collection of primary and secondary works on seven British writers including Dorothy L Sayers and G K Chesterton. Publishes annual review, *Seven*. Holdings include books, manuscripts, periodicals, artwork, photographs, and audio/video tapes.

Entertainment & Gifts

ACORN MEDIA

801 Roeder Rd Ste 700	FAX	1-301-608-9312
Silver Spring MD 20910-4468 USA	TOLLFREE	1-800-474-2277
	EMAIL	info@acornmedia.com
	WEBSITE	www.acornmedia.com

〜 Source for videos & DVDs of several mystery series, including Ian Carmichael as Lord Peter Wimsey, Derek Jacobi as Brother Cadfael, David Suchet as Hercule Poirot. Secure online ordering or call toll-free.

☞ AUDIBLE

PHONE	1-973-890-8799
TOLLFREE	1-888-429-5575
WEBSITE	www.audible.com

〜 Download audiobooks for your MP3 player, PocketPC, or computer. Abridged and unabridged audio in original publisher's editions. Prices much lower than cassettes or CDs; save even more with club membership (not required).

☞ THE AUDIO PARTNERS PUBLISHING CORP.

1133 High St	PHONE	1-530-480-7804
Auburn CA 95603 USA	TOLLFREE	1-888-480-7803
	EMAIL	info@audiopartners.com
	WEBSITE	www.audiopartners.com

〜 Publishes over 100 unabridged mysteries in their "Mystery Masters" line. Authors include Agatha Christie, Rex Stout, Ellery Queen, Ellis Peters, Georges Simenon, Dick Francis and many more. Committed to superb readers, quality production, and gift-quality packaging.

AUDIO-PLAYWRIGHTS

Hal Glatzer	PHONE	1-415-487-0720
1421 Oak St	FAX	1-415-431-9516
San Francisco CA 94117-2117 USA	EMAIL	hal@audio-play.com
	WEBSITE	www.audio-play.com

〜 Produces full-cast audio-plays with high production values. Katy Green mystery series set in 1940s with swing music and songs.

THE AUSTIN HILL INN

Debbie & John Bailey, Innkeepers	PHONE	1-802-464-5281
Route 100	FAX	1-802-464-1229
PO Box 859	TOLLFREE	1-800-332-7352
West Dover VT 05356-0859 USA	EMAIL	austinhi@sover.net
	WEBSITE	www.austinhillinn.com

An 11-rm bed and breakfast inn that hosts murder mystery weekends throughout the year. Reservations available for individual rooms or the entire inn.

BOGIE'S MYSTERY TOURS®

Karen & Bill Palmer, Owners	PHONE	1-212-362-7569
328 W 86th St Ste 4A	EMAIL	BMT@Bogies.net
New York NY 10024-3124 USA	WEBSITE	www.Bogies.net/bmt.html

🎭 Interactive mystery events since 1981, by the creators of Mystery Dinner Theater. "Our mysteries are perfect for special events and entertainment."

BOOK ADVENTURES

Mary Lou White, President	FL PHONE/FAX	1-941-480-0074
Nov-Apr:	OH PHONE/FAX	1-937-434-9019
512 W Venice Ave #102	EMAIL	BookAdvent@aol.com
Venice FL 34285-2017 USA	WEBSITE	www.bookadventures.com
May-Oct:		
7111 Fallen Oak Trace		
Centerville OH 45459-4845 USA		

🎭 Travel with companions who love to read. International literary tours. **Jun 25–Jul 9, 2003:** Celtic Trails in Wales, Cornwall and Brittany; **October, 2003:** Jane Austen Tours in England.

BOOKCRAZY RADIO

Debbie Neckel	PHONE	1-623-583-7567
9800 W Peoria Ave Ste 2	EMAIL	iambookcrazy@aol.com
Peoria AZ 85345 USA	WEBSITE	www.bookcrazy.net

🎭 The first 24/7 book radio on the Internet. All genres from romance to SF to literature to mystery. Weekly mystery hour; author interviews frequently feature mystery writers. Requires Windows Media Player.

BOOKS IN MOTION

9922 E Montgomery Ste 31	TOLLFREE	1-800-752-3199
Spokane WA 99206 USA	EMAIL	sales@booksinmotion.com
	WEBSITE	www.booksinmotion.com

〰 Publisher of unabridged audiobooks. Buy or rent. Secure online ordering. Also available at many truck stops—rent tapes at one location, return them at another.

BOOKS ON TAPE®

PO Box 25122	PHONE	1-714-825-0021
Santa Ana CA 92799-5122 USA	FAX	1-714-825-0756
	TOLLFREE	1-800-88-BOOKS
	EMAIL	botcs@booksontape.com
	WEBSITE	www.booksontape.com

〰 Unabridged audiobooks for rent or purchase. Many classic older mysteries as well as new releases. Catalog, email newsletter.

BRILLIANCE AUDIOBOOKS

1704 Eaton Dr	PHONE	1-616-846-5256
Grand Haven MI 49417 USA	FAX	1-616-846-0630
	TOLLFREE	1-800-854-7859
	EMAIL	service@brillianceaudio.com
	WEBSITE	www.brillianceaudio.com
	WEBSITE	www.audiobookstand.com

Unabridged (and a few abridged) books on audio cassettes, at reasonable prices. Bookcassette brand offers twice as much audio on a single tape. Email newsletter.

BRODART

500 Arch St	FAX	1-800-283-6087
PO Box 3037	TOLLFREE	1-888-820-4377
Williamsport PA 17705-0001 USA	EMAIL	bookinfo@brodart.com
	WEBSITE	www.brodart.com

Maker of archival-quality book jacket covers and other library supplies. Essential care for your book collection.

CRUISES TO DIE FOR

Paulina Noel & Sherry Leybovich	EMAIL	info@cruisestodiefor.com
3077 Azelea Sands Lane	WEBSITE	www.cruisestodiefor.com
Dumfries VA 22026 USA		

Each murder mystery is individually written with the particular ship, itinerary and guests in mind. Hosting the Mystery Writers Forum at Sea, June 29–July 6, 2003.

DASTARDLY DUSTJACKET JEWELRY

Diane Plumley	PHONE	1-718-545-4624
3011 34th St #5E	EMAIL	finsbry@aol.com
Astoria NY 11103-5148 USA	WEBSITE	home.att.net/~csilberblatt/jewelry.htm

Hand-crafted pins, earrings, and other jewelry incorporating reproductions of vintage mystery book covers, along with charms and crystals. Will do custom orders for mystery authors.

DOUBLEDOG PRESS

Janet Dickey	EMAIL	doubledog@core.com
PO Box 46826	WEBSITE	dbldog.com
Bedford OH 44146-0826 USA		

Kits that enable librarians and other youth leaders to produce mystery programs for teens or children (grades 3–5).

EDDIE MAY MYSTERIES

	PHONE	1-613-729-8832
	TOLLFREE	1-877-WE-SLAY-U
	EMAIL	murder@eddiemay.com
	WEBSITE	www.eddiemay.com

Scheduled performances at the Marble Works restaurant and custom events for private parties. In Ottawa, Ontario, since 1984. Other troupes across North America.

FEMMES FATALES: A CATALOG OF MYSTERY GIFTS

Marisa Babjak	PHONE	1-562-924-6711
PO Box 3457	FAX	1-562-809-1892
Lakewood CA 90712-3457 USA	TOLLFREE	1-800-596-DEAD
	EMAIL	byteocrime@aol.com
	WEBSITE	www.mysterygifts.biz

Everything you can imagine and more—ties, filmstrips, games, cards, sculpture, jewelry, handcuffs, hats, books, and even gift coffins. Also wholesale to book and gift stores.

GET-A-CLUE PRODUCTIONS

Kelli Connors, Owner/Producer	PHONE	1-603-330-9928
PO Box 433	PHONE	1-207-793-2761
Rollinsford NH 03869-0433 USA	EMAIL	info@get-a-clue-productions.com
	WEBSITE	www.get-a-clue-productions.com

Traveling entertainment company specializing in interactive musical murder mysteries. Also theme nights, live game shows, specialty acts and children's musicals. Custom events planning for groups of 10-300.

HALEY PRODUCTIONS' INTERACTIVE CHALLENGES

Susan Haley	PHONE/FAX	1-415-456-3302
75 Elizabeth Way	TOLLFREE	1-800-293-3302
San Rafael CA 94901-1151 USA	EMAIL	susan@haleyproductions.com
	WEBSITE	www.haleyproductions.com

Interactive murder mysteries, scavenger hunts and team building for any event. Do-it-yourself murder mystery games, team building games and scavenger hunts also available.

HAMMETT'S SAN FRANCISCO

Don Herron	PHONE	1-510-287-9540
	EMAIL	dashdude@donherron.com
	WEBSITE	www.donherron.com

Travel over the fog-shrouded hills stalked by Sam Spade, the Continental Op, and other legendary characters created by San Francisco's most renowned mystery writer. See website or call for dates and times.

HARRY PACKER MANSION

Pat & Bob Handwerk	PHONE	1-570-325-8566
PO Box 458	EMAIL	mystery@murdermansion.com
Jim Thorpe PA 18229-3458 USA	WEBSITE	www.murdermansion.com

Murder mystery weekends at a restored Victorian bed & breakfast, used as a model for the Haunted Mansion at Disney World. Named the Best Murder Mystery on the East Coast by Condé Nast.

Jewelry To Die For

Barbara Riccardi Bernstein
548 North St
Greene NY 13778-2115 USA
   Handmade jewelry with mystery themes.

The Killing Kompany

Jon Avner

PHONE	1-212-772-2590
TOLLFREE	1-888-SHOOT-EM
EMAIL	killingkompany@killingkompany.com
WEBSITE	www.killingkompany.com

   Interactive murder mystery dinner theater. Scheduled shows and private events.

Lance Entertainment

Radio City Station
PO Box 931
New York NY 10101-0931 USA

PHONE	1-212-471-0247
FAX	1-212-247-2679
TOLLFREE	1-800-690-8161
EMAIL	lancehq@lanceentertainment.com
WEBSITE	www.lanceentertainment.com

   Videocassettes and DVDs of previously produced, high-quality mystery entertainment from writers such as Dick Francis, P. D. James, Georges Simenon, and Ruth Rendell.

The Lizzie Borden Bed & Breakfast / Museum

Martha McGinn & Simone J Evans
92 2nd St
Fall River MA 02721-2006 USA

PHONE	1-508-675-7333
EMAIL	lizziebnb@lizzie-borden.com
WEBSITE	www.lizzie-borden.com

   Restored former residence of the Borden family. Lizzie Borden and Fall River memorabilia. Tours & gift shop. Guest rooms for those who dare to spend the night.

LTF Studios

Lola Troy Fiur
360 E 65th St #17a
New York NY 10021-6724 USA

PHONE/FAX	1-212-861-1911
EMAIL	ltfoto@bellatlantic.net

   Original notecards, T-shirts, & photographs with mystery themes. Featuring Sherlock Holmes, Nancy Drew, "Poison", and authors of the Golden Age & 1940s.

Mohonk Mystery Weekend

Michelle Woodruff
Mohonk Mountain House
1000 Mountain Rest Rd
New Paltz NY 12561-2814 USA

PHONE	1-914-255-1000
FAX	1-914-256-2100
TOLLFREE	1-800-772-6646
WEBSITE	www.mohonk.com

   One of the originals. Murder weekends with guest authors taking part, since 1978.

MOSTLY MURDER

Art Feinglass, Writer/Producer	PHONE	1-212-581-8655
61 W 62nd St #25A	FAX	1-212-245-5953
New York NY 10023-7023 USA	EMAIL	mostlymurd@aol.com
	WEBSITE	www.mostlymurder.com

🕯 Murder mystery entertainment that gets you into the act. Corporate events, birthday & anniversary parties, fund raisers, bar/bat mitzvah parties. NY, NJ, & CT: ask for free demo video.

MURDER AT THE LIBRARY

Penny & Tom Warner	PHONE	1-925-837-7089
710 Sinnet Ct	FAX	1-925-820-5478
Danville CA 94526-5537 USA	EMAIL	tpwarner@ix.netcom.com

🕯 Murder mystery scripts & props designed especially for libraries and their fundraising. Est. 1987.

MURDER BY INVITATION

Harriet & Larry Stay	PHONE	1-360-765-4432
PO Box 1201	EMAIL	stays@olypen.com
Port Townsend WA 98368-0901		
USA		

🕯 Est. 1984. Participatory theater company, mystery weekends & corporate events.

MURDER INK PRODUCTIONS

Marney & Alan Austin	PHONE/FAX	1-602-952-8447
	EMAIL	info@murderinkproductions.com
	WEBSITE	www.murderinkproductions.com

🕯 AKA Arizona Performing Arts Theatre. Mystery dinners for groups from 15 to 300, Phoenix area. Mystery weekends at historic Arizona hotels.

MURDER MYSTERY INC.

Ron & Joni Pacie	PHONE	1-631-673-4979
18 Hollywood Pl	FAX	1-631-549-3252
Huntington NY 11743-4201 USA	TOLLFREE	1-800-MURDER INC
	EMAIL	info@murdermysteryinc.com
	WEBSITE	www.murdermysteryinc.com

🕯 Experts at producing "killer" evenings, weekends, events, fundraisers, cruises. Over a decade of experience creating interactive murder mysteries nationally & internationally. When in NY visit the Off-Broadway Comedy Mystery Dinner Theater.

MURDER ON THE MENU®

Janet A Rudolph, Writer/Producer	PHONE	1-510-845-3600
7155 Marlborough Ter	FAX	1-510-845-1975
Berkeley CA 94705-1736 USA	WEBSITE	www.murderonthemenu.com
	EMAIL	whodunit@murderonthemenu.com

🕯 Customized interactive murder mystery events as entertainment and team-building for meetings, incentives, private parties, and conventions, anywhere in the world.

Murder on the Menu (UK)

Gerri Smith & Terry Victor	PHONE	+44 7000 M4MURDER
10 Canon Lane	FAX	+44 2920 734398
Caerwent, Monmouthshire	EMAIL	tv@murderonthemenu.co.uk
NP6 4QQ WALES	WEBSITE	www.murderonthemenu.co.uk

🎭 Fully professional interactive mystery entertainment and over 30 cabaret whodunnits for corporate or private events. Scheduled and bespoke (custom) murder mysteries. Preferred suppliers to the *Orient Express* and *Northern Belle* trains and *DFDS SS Scandinavian Princess*. Member of the Meetings Industry Association.

Murder To Go

David Landau, President	PHONE	1-973-301-0562
92 Ridgedale Ave	EMAIL	murdertogo@att.net
Florham Park NJ 07932-2007 USA	WEBSITE	www.murder-to-go.com

🎭 Est. 1982. Operates dinner theaters, licenses scripts, produces corporate entertainment worldwide. Products include interactive DVD games, party games, a mystery card game, board game, and direct-to-DVD interactive feature film mysteries.

Murderer Among Us

James Donohoe	PHONE	1-510-525-2160
5645 Broadway Ste 100	EMAIL	murderer_among_us@yahoo.com
Oakland CA 94618 USA	WEBSITE	www.mysteryfun.com

🎭 Customized murder mystery parties for groups of 12–200. No actors—all parts are played by guests.

MurderWatch® Mystery Theatre

Connie & Jeff Gay	PHONE	1-407-850-9555
Dreamland Productions	EMAIL	murderwatch@cfl.rr.com
PO Box 771177	WEBSITE	www.murderwatch.com
Orlando FL 32877-1177 USA		

🎭 Musical murder-mystery dinner shows and game shows at Walt Disney World's Grosvenor Resort Hotel. Additional location in St. Augustine, FL, opening in Feb 2003. Also, murder mysteries on audiocassette.

Mysteries and More

54 N Big Oak Dr	PHONE	1-828-681-8182
Fletcher SC 28732 USA	FAX	1-828-684-6463
	TOLLFREE	1-888-346-0777
	EMAIL	customer_service@murdermysterygames.com
	WEBSITE	www.murdermysterygames.com

🕸 Carries a complete lineup of mystery games and puzzles for all ages. Secure online ordering.

MYSTERIES BY MOUSHEY, INC.

Eileen Moushey	PHONE	1-330-678-3893
PO Box 3593	FAX	1-330-434-9376
Kent OH 44240-0046 USA	EMAIL	info@mysteriesbymoushey.com
	WEBSITE	www.mysteriesbymoushey.com

Lighthearted audience-participation mysteries, professionally staged. Scripts available for your own production.

MYSTERIES BY VINCENT

Cindy Vincent	TOLLFREE	1-866-WHODUNIT
3506 Hwy 6 South, PMB 101	EMAIL	cindy@mysteriesbyvincent.com
Sugarland TX 77478-4401 USA	WEBSITE	www.mysteriesbyvincent.com

Mystery party games for 8 or 10 guests, ranging from very-easy-to-host to games for more elaborate parties. Special line of games for women only, and the Daisy Diamond Detective Series™ for pre-teen girls. Interactive Mystery Party Skit-kits™ for large groups, fundraisers and B & Bs. Games and Skit-kits™ contain complete instructions.

THE MYSTERIOUS PEN

Bill Creed, Producer	PHONE	1-301-913-9071
Duet Communications	FAX	1-301-913-9072
3404 Kenilworth Dr	EMAIL	billc@mysteriouspen.com
Chevy Chase MD 20815-4722 USA	WEBSITE	www.mysteriouspen.com

Series of video interviews with well-known mystery writers, discussing the craft of writing and their writing careers. Each 1-hr video features a different author, interviewed by Bill Creed, an Emmy-nominated video producer/editor and longtime mystery fan.

MYSTERIOUSLY YOURS... MYSTERY DINNER THEATER

Brian Caws	PHONE	1-416-486-7469
2026 Yonge St	FAX	1-416-486-7822
Toronto ON M4S 1Z9 CANADA	TOLLFREE	1-800-NOT-DEAD
	EMAIL	info@MysteriouslyYours.com
	WEBSITE	www.MysteriouslyYours.com

Interactive murder mystery dinner theater and matinees in Toronto, as well as private, customized mysteries and corporate, team-building programs & parties.

MYSTERY BY DESIGN

Katie Hassett	PHONE	1-408-266-7194
1341 Duke Way	FAX	1-408-267-6731
San Jose CA 95125-3917 USA	EMAIL	mbd@pacbell.net
	WEBSITE	www.mysterybydesign.com

Writes & produces scripted interactive mysteries and other types of original interactive presentations for any event: team building, conference, convention, new product introduction, meeting, holidays, birthday, fund raiser. Dialog is customized to clients' requirements. Will rent scripts to distant groups. In Green Valley, AZ, call 1-520-648-6139; in Salt Lake City, call 1-801-495-2583.

MYSTERY CAFÉ DINNER THEATER (BOSTON MA)

David Goldstein	PHONE	1-617-423-1999
	TOLLFREE	1-800-697-CLUE
	EMAIL	david@comedytheater.com
	WEBSITE	www.comedytheater.com

※ Dinner theater in Boston and traveling troupe in all New England States. Boston Harbor mystery cruises Jun–Dec. Mansion mysteries Jan–May.

MYSTERY CAFÉ (INDIANAPOLIS IN)

Joseph Strange, Prod Manager	PHONE	1-317-684-0668
201 S College Ave	FAX	1-317-684-0348
Indianapolis IN 46202 USA	EMAIL	info@themysterycafeindy.com
	WEBSITE	www.themysterycafeindy.com

※ At the Milano Inn & private parties. Four acts and four courses.

MYSTERY EVENTS

Grahame Parkyn Smith	PHONE	+44 1727 759 631
129 Green Lane	EMAIL	Grahame@mysteryevents.co.uk
Saint Albans, Herts AL3 6HG	WEBSITE	www.mysteryevents.co.uk
ENGLAND		

※ Group participation mystery events for 12–150 people. Specialists in corporate entertainment.

MYSTERY PARTY KITS

David & Susan Given-Seymour	PHONE	1-360-966-4297
PO Box 4052	EMAIL	mariner@orcawatch.com
Nooksack WA 98276-0052 USA		

※ Kits designed with all the materials you need to do your own party, as a fundraiser or just for fun. Roles provided for up to 80 guests.

THE MYSTERY SHOP

Mary Heitert	PHONE	1-630-690-1105
551 Sundance Ct	FAX	1-630-690-7928
Carol Stream IL 60188-9211 USA	EMAIL	tms@TheMysteryShop.com
	WEBSITE	www.themysteryshop.com

※ Live theatre company specializing in adult and children's participatory mysteries. All ages, all groups.

☞ THE NOSTALGIA FACTORY

Rudy & Barbara Franchi	PHONE	1-617-241-8300
Charlestown Commerce Center	FAX	1-617-241-0710
50 Terminal St, Bldg 2	TOLLFREE	1-800-479-8754
Boston MA 02129 USA	EMAIL	posters@nostalgia.com
	WEBSITE	www.nostalgia.com

✎ Original movie posters & related ephemera. Over 36,000 items. Online searchable database with secure ordering. Oldest and largest movie poster site on the web.

NOVEL EXPLORATIONS

Patty Suchy	PHONE	1-410-992-6656
4785 Dorsey Hall Dr Ste 102	FAX	1-410-964-0878
Ellicott City MD 21042 USA	TOLLFREE	1-800-432-6659
	EMAIL	novelexp@comcast.net
	WEBSITE	www.novelexplorations.com

🎭 Literary & research travel for readers and writers. Features mystery tours of Great Britain, occasional cruises. Group specialist for travel fundraising events with literary or research theme. British Tourist Authority Destination Specialist.

PC DESIGN

Jeffrey Luther	FAX	1-650-326-9925
PO Box 417	EMAIL	pcdesign@pulpcards.com
Palo Alto CA 93024 USA	WEBSITE	www.pulpcards.com

Vintage paperback & pulp fiction cover art reproduced on postcards, T-shirts, coffee mugs, mousepads, tote bags, more. 312 designs. Free digital postcards. Catalog available. Online ordering.

RECORDED BOOKS®

270 Skipjack Rd	FAX	1-410-535-5499
Prince Frederick MD 20678-3410	TOLLFREE	1-800-638-1304
USA	EMAIL	recordedbooks@recordedbooks.com
	WEBSITE	www.recordedbooks.com

Unabridged audiobooks for sale or rent. Over 2500 titles, not available in stores. Online ordering. Email newsletter.

RED HERRING PRODUCTIONS

Mike Stevens	WEBSITE	www.redherringproductions.com
838 Pleasant St		
Colorado Springs CO 80904-1509		
USA		

🎭 Corporate entertainment, murder mystery shows, historical characters and theme training for groups of 20–500. Est. 1985.

SCENARIO PRODUCTIONS

Mark Bornstein	PHONE	1-416-539-0673
831 Glencairn Ave, Suite 276	EMAIL	brick@scenarioproductions.com
Toronto ON M6B 2A4 CANADA	WEBSITE	www.scenarioproductions.com

Creators of Brick Mallery, Private Investigator. Full-cast audio dramas available on cassette. New productions of vintage CBC radio Mystery Theatre.

SHERLOCK HOLMES MEMORABILIA COMPANY

230 Baker St
London NW1 5RT ENGLAND

PHONE +44 20 7486 1426
FAX +44 20 7935 0522
EMAIL sales@shmc.demon.co.uk
WEBSITE www.sh-memorabilia.co.uk

§ Assorted Sherlockian gift items, collectible books and magazines. Open shop at the location of "The Empty House," with exhibition of the set from the Granada TV series with Jeremy Brett. Catalog and on-line sales.

SKELETONS IN THE CLOSET

LA County Dept of Coroner
1104 N Mission Rd
Los Angeles CA 90033-1096 USA

PHONE 1-323-343-0760
FAX 1-323-342-9106
WEBSITE www.lacoroner.com

Official L.A. County Coroner merchandise. Clothing, office items, mugs, and more. Open shop, catalog available. Proceeds go to the Youthful Drunk Driving Visitation Program.

STAGE SHADOWS MYSTERY THEATRE CO.

Esmee, Senior Producer
PO Box 900
New York NY 10185-0900 USA

PHONE 1-212-604-4612
EMAIL stageshadows@hotmail.com
WEBSITE www.stageshadows.com

"Radio Like You've Never Seen It." Classic radio mysteries & original dramas taped live in front of a studio audience at New York City's Museum of Television & Radio and broadcast at a future date.

SUSPICIOUS ACTS: MADE TO ORDER

Jean & Adam Sloan

PHONE 1-810-463-9777
EMAIL jeansloan@worldnet.att.net
WEBSITE home.att.net/~jeansloan/

Mystery events for corporations, organizations, country clubs & The Grand Hotel, Mackinac Island, Michigan.

T-SHIRTS BY STU SHIFFMAN

Stu Shiffman
8616 Linden Ave N
Seattle WA 98103-3926 USA

PHONE 1-206-522-1262
WEBSITE www.drizzle.com/~roscoe/tshirts.html
EMAIL roscoe@drizzle.com

Mystery and Sherlockian-theme T-shirts by a well-known fan and illustrator.

THEATRE OF INTERACTIVE DRAMA

Alan Lance Andersen
122 West Ash Lane
Roland IA 50236 USA

PHONE/FAX 1-515-388-5573
EMAIL andersen@interdrama.com
WEBSITE www.interdrama.com

Audience-participation mystery dramas include historical re-creations.

TIME AND MATERIALS

Susan Castle
334D Payran St
Petaluma CA 94952-3208 USA

PHONE 1-707-769-1729

🦋 Mystery jewelry: mixed media collage brooches with watch faces and parts, hardware and charms.

VIDEO PREVIEW COLLECTION

4828 Park Glen Rd
Minneapolis MN 55416 USA

FAX 1-310-399-4844
TOLLFREE 1-800-771-9232
WEBSITE www.VideoPreview.com

〰 Catalog includes several mystery movies and miniseries first aired on A&E or PBS.

VILLAGE STORYTAPES

Debby Mackintosh, Owner
PO Box 1440
Sebastopol CA 95473-1440 USA

FAX 1-707-823-1128
TOLLFREE 1-800-238-TAPE
EMAIL human@storytapes.com
WEBSITE www.storytapes.com

〰 Unabridged and abridged audiobooks for sale or rent. Large mystery selection. Discount plans, gift certificates.

WHODUNIT PRODUCTIONS

Shauna Hoffman
26893 Bouquet Canyon Rd #113
Santa Clarita CA 91350-2374 USA

PHONE 1-661-297-3208
EMAIL suspect@whodunitcruises.com
WEBSITE whodunitcruises.com
WEBSITE murdermysterycruise.com

🎭 Whodunit Productions has become partners in crime with Royal Caribbean Cruise Lines in creating "Murder on the High Seas!" We have 3, 5 and 7-night mystery cruises traveling to Mexico, Caribbean and Alaska in 2003. Join us if you dare.... Custom corporate cruise events also available.

THE WORLD OF A&E

PO Box 2284
South Burlington VT 05407-2284
　　USA

TOLLFREE 1-888-423-1212
WEBSITE www.AandEcatalog.com

〰 Source for videos and DVDs of many detective series which aired in the US on A&E, plus classic TV series such as *The Prisoner*. Special Nero Wolfe Shop.

Awards

AGATHA AWARDS

WEBSITE   www.malicedomestic.org/agatha.htm

♟ Voted on by the **Malice Domestic** convention attendees, for the best traditional mysteries of the previous year. Named for Agatha Christie, exemplary writer of classic mysteries. Presentation in the form of a teapot.

ANTHONY AWARDS

♟ Nominees and winners selected by attendees of **Bouchercon** World Mystery Convention. Award named for the late Anthony Boucher (William Anthony Parker White), well-known writer, critic, and fan of the mystery genre. Each convention committee designs its own award to present to the winners.

ARTHUR ELLIS AWARDS

WEBSITE   www.crimewriterscanada.com

♟ Presented by the **Crime Writers of Canada** to honour the best works published by Canadian authors during the previous year. Arthur Ellis was the **nom de travail** of Canada's official hangman (now unemployed). The statuette consists of a wooden gallows with a puppet suspended from it. If you pull the cord attached to the puppet it "dances" on the rope.

BARRY AWARDS

WEBSITE   www.deadlypleasures.com/Barry.htm

♟ Nominees and winners selected by readers of **Deadly Pleasures** magazine. Award est. 1998 and named in honor of notable fan Barry Gardner.

CARTIER DIAMOND DAGGER AWARD

WEBSITE   www.thecwa.co.uk

♟ Given by the **Crime Writers Association** for outstanding contribution to the genre. The Cartier Diamond Dagger is worth £30,000 and emerges from the Cartier vaults only once a year for the awards ceremony. Though no crime writer keeps the Diamond Dagger, Cartier presents each winner with a superb Diamond Dagger brooch or cufflinks.

CHESTER HIMES MYSTERY AWARDS

♟ Given to a published African American Mystery Writer and to the winner of the local Oakland Unified School District student writing contest. Awarded at the annual **Chester Himes Mystery Writers Conference**, in Oakland, California.

CLUE OF THE YEAR

♟ Award given by the **Suomen Dekkariseura**, the Finnish Whodunnit Society, for the best crime novel or achievement related to the field

DAGGER AWARDS

WEBSITE   www.thecwa.co.uk

☙ The **Crime Writers Association** (UK) announces the Dagger awards in December, for works published between 16 Oct of the previous year and 15 Oct of the award year. Each category is judged by independent committee appointed by the CWA. Awards co-sponsored by The Macallan.

DAVITT AWARD

WEBSITE   home.vicnet.net.au/~sincoz/scarlet.htm

☙ Given by **Sisters in Crime Australia** for the best crime novel by an Australian woman in the previous year. Named after Australia's first crime novelist, Ellen Davitt.

DERRICK MURDOCH AWARD

WEBSITE   www.crimewriterscanada.com

☙ Given by the **Crime Writers of Canada** to recognize outstanding contribution to the genre of crime writing in Canada. Named for reviewer Derrick Murdoch, one of the founders of the CWC.

DERRINGER AWARDS

☙ Nominations and awards voted on by members of the **Short Mystery Fiction Society**. Award established in 1998, named to emphasize the short but deadly nature of the mystery fiction honored. Winners receive a certificate depicting the eponymous weapon.

DEUTSCHE KRIMI PREIS

WEBSITE   homepages.compuserve.de/krimijahn/dkp/dkp-all.htm

☙ Oldest mystery award in Germany, from **BKA: Bochumer Krimi Archiv**. Decided by an independent jury of literary scholars, reviewers, critics and booksellers. Awarded each January for the three best detective novels of the year before, in two categories, national and international.

DILYS AWARD

WEBSITE   www.mysterybooksellers.com/dilys.html

☙ Awarded by the **Independent Mystery Booksellers Association**, for the book that was the most fun to sell. Award named for Dilys Winn, founder of the mystery bookstore Murder Ink.

EDGAR ALLAN POE AWARDS

WEBSITE   www.mysterywriters.org/awards.html

☙ Awarded by the **Mystery Writers of America** in April of each year. Award named for the writer of the first detective story, a bust of whom is given to the winners. Each category is judged by a committee of MWA members.

ELLEN NEHR AWARD

WEBSITE   www.acwl.org/nehr.htm

☙ Given by the **American Crime Writers League** to show appreciation for mystery reviewers who demonstrate a solid knowledge of the field and give an unbiased and informed criticism of each work. Named for the late fan and critic Ellen Nehr.

Ellery Queen Award

WEBSITE   www.mysterywriters.org/awards.html

Occasionally given by the **Mystery Writers of America** to honor writing teams or outstanding individuals in the mystery publishing field. Named for the pseudonym used by Frederic Dannay and Manfred Lee as mystery writers, editors, and critics.

Ellis Peters Historical Dagger

WEBSITE   www.thecwa.co.uk

Given by the **Crime Writers Association.** Nominees must have a crime theme and a historical background of any place or period up to 1965. The Historical Dagger comes with a prize of £2,000.

Falcon

WEBSITE   www.asahi-net.or.jp/~AP9T-AMN/falcon/faward1.html

Award given by **The Maltese Falcon Society** of Japan.

Glass Key

Awarded by the **Crime Writers of Scandinavia,** for the best Scandinavian mystery of the previous year. The award is an actual glass key.

Glauser & Ehrenglauser

WEBSITE   www.das-syndikat.com/glauser.htm

Award given by **Das Syndikat,** the German Crime Writers Association. The Glauser is awarded for best novel of the year and the Ehrenglauser is given for lifetime achievement. The Glauser carries a prize of 10,000 marks.

Gouden Strop

WEBSITE   www.crime.nl/frames/prijzen-frame.html

Golden Noose, awarded for the best Dutch crime novel. Est 1986 by the Genootschap Nederlandstalige Misdaadauteurs (Dutch Crime Writers Association). Winner is selected by an independent jury.

Grand Master Award

WEBSITE   www.mysterywriters.org/awards.html

Given by the **Mystery Writers of America** to recognize not only important contributions to the mystery field over time, but a significant output of consistently high quality as well.

La Grand Prix de Littérateur Policière

France's highest award for crime writing, established in 1948.

Hammett Prize

Awarded by the **North American Branch of the International Association of Crime Writers,** for a work of literary excellence in the field of crime writing, by a US or Canadian author. The winning title is chosen by a group of three distinguished outside judges, and the winner receives a bronze "Thin Man" trophy.

Herodotus Awards

WEBSITE mywebpages.comcast.net/monkshould/herodotus.html

Presented by the **Historical Mystery Appreciation Society** for best historical mystery writing in six categories. Named for the 5th c. (BC) historian who narrated events in the manner of a storyteller.

Ian Fleming Steel Dagger

WEBSITE www.thecwa.co.uk

Annual prize for thriller, adventure, or spy fiction novel. Sponsored by Ian Fleming Publications Ltd. and awarded by the Crime Writers Association.

John Creasey Memorial Dagger

WEBSITE www.thecwa.co.uk

Awarded annually by **Crime Writer's Association** of Great Britain, since 1973, for the best first crime novel published in the UK in English by an author who has not previously published a full-length novel of any sort. Named for the author John Creasey, one of the founders of the Crime Writer's Association. The award of £750 is sponsored by Chivers Press.

Lambda Literary Awards for Mystery

WEBSITE www.lambdalit.org/lammy/

Awarded by the Lambda Literary Foundation, publishers of the *Lambda Book Report*, for the best gay men's mystery and best lesbian mystery. Lammies are also given in 18 other categories.

Lefty Award

Given by the **Left Coast Crime** convention for the most humorous book of the year. Not given every year.

Macavity Awards

WEBSITE www.mysteryreaders.org/Macavity.html

Awards nominated and voted on by members of **Mystery Readers International**. Award named for Macavity, the mystery cat, from T.S. Eliot's *Old Possum's Book of Practical Cats*. Winners receive a certificate and a stuffed cat representing the elusive Macavity.

Marlowe Award

Award given by the **Raymond Chandler Gesellschaft**. Named for Chandlers famous sleuth, Philip Marlowe.

Martin Beck Award

Given by the **Svenska Deckarakademin** in two categories: best Swedish crime novel, and best foreign crime novel translated into Swedish. Named for the police detective character created by Maj Sjöwall and Per Wahlöö.

Mary Higgins Clark Award

WEBSITE   www.mysterywriters.org/awards.html

♟ Given by the **Mystery Writers of America** for the book written most closely in the Mary Higgins Clark tradition of romantic suspense. Nominees are chosen from those sent to the Edgar Committees for Best Novel, Best First Novel and Best Paperback Novel. The winner is selected by a special MWA committee. Sponsored by Simon & Schuster.

Ned Kelly Awards

WEBSITE   www.thecwaa.net

♟ The **Crime Writers' Association of Australia** established the Ned Kelly Awards in 1996. They are named for a notorious Australian outlaw of the 19th century, and affectionately called the Neddies.

Nero Wolfe Award

WEBSITE   www.nerowolfe.org

♟ Given by **The Wolfe Pack** for the novel that best reflects the Nero Wolfe tradition in detective writing. Presented at their Black Orchid Dinner in December of each year.

Palle Rosenkrantz Award

♟ Given by **Det Danske Kriminalakademi** for the best Danish crime novel of the year. Named for the Danish author (1867-1941). Selected by an independent jury. Diplomas are given in additional categories, such as best first novel, TV series, etc.

Raven Award

WEBSITE   www.mysterywriters.org/awards.html

♟ Occasionally given by the **Mystery Writers of America** to honor outstanding achievement in the mystery field outside the realm of creative writing. Past awards have been given for Reader of the Year and for book jacket design.

Robert L Fish Memorial Award

WEBSITE   www.mysterywriters.org/awards.html

♟ Given by the **Mystery Writers of America** for the best first short story by an American author. Co-sponsored by the Robert L Fish estate.

Romantic Times Reviewers' Choice Awards

WEBSITE   www.romantictimes.com/b_books/awards.shtml

♟ Since 1999, the reviewers at **Romantic Times BOOKclub** give Mystery & Suspense awards in six categories.

Scarlet Stiletto Award

WEBSITE   home.vicnet.net.au/~sincoz/scarlet.htm

♟ Given by **Sisters in Crime Australia** to the winner of a short story competition for women resident in Australia.

Shamus Awards

WEBSITE   www.execpc.com/~piesbook/awardwinners.html

♟ Given by the **Private Eye Writers of America** to honor excellent work in the Private Eye genre. The PWA defines a "private eye" as any mystery protagonist who is a paid investigator, but not a police officer or government agent.

SHERLOCK AWARDS

WEBSITE   www.pmh.uk.com/sherlock/sherlock.htm

♟ Given by **Sherlock Holmes, The Detective Magazine,** for distinctive detectives in several categories.

SPOTTED OWL AWARD

WEBSITE   www.friendsofmystery.org/award.html

♟ From **Friends of Mystery,** for the best mystery book written by a writer of the Pacific Northwest (Alaska, British Columbia, Idaho, Oregon, and Washington).

Appendix

CHRONOLOGICAL LIST OF EVENTS
2003

Jan 1–Dec 31	Wallonie 2003, Année Simenon au Pays de Liège
Feb 7–9	Love Is Murder
Feb 8	Murder in the Magic City
Feb 28–Mar 2	Left Coast Crime 2003
Mar 13–16	SleuthFest
Mar 28–30	Bare Bones Writers Retreat
May 2–4	Malice Domestic XV
May 9–18	Daphne du Maurier Festival of Arts and Literature
May 5	Festival of Mystery
May 14–18	Die Criminale
May 16–17	Chester Himes Mystery Writers Conference
May 29–Jun 1	Mayhem in the Midlands
May 30–31	Murder in the Grove
Summer	Festival du Roman Noir
Jun 1	No Crime Unpublished™
Jun 13–14	Deadly Ink Mystery Conference
Jun 13–15	Bloody Words
Jun 14	Of Dark and Stormy Nights
Jun 14	Flatirons Blunt Instruments
Jun 28–Jul 27	WMU Prague Summer Program: Crime Fiction Workshop
July	Semana Negra
July	Crime Scene
Jul 17–20	Book Passage Mystery Writers' Conference
Jul 17–20	Harrowgate Crime Writers Festival
Jul 18–19	Harriette Austin Writers Conference
Jul 18–20	ClueFest 12
Aug 21–Sep 8	British Mystery & Crime Writers Program: London and Oxford
Sep 3–14	Cozy Crimes, Cream Teas & Books, Books, Books
Sep 5–7	St Hilda's Crime & Mystery Weekend
Sep 7	NYC Collectible Paperback & Pulp Fiction Expo
Sep 13–15	Colorado Gold Writers Conference
October	Dead on Deansgate
Oct 5–11	Mystery Series Week
Oct 16–19	Bouchercon 2003
Oct 24–26	Magna Cum Murder
Oct 31–Nov 2	Cape Fear Crime Festival

2004

Feb 19–22	Left Coast Crime 2004
Mar 6–13	Murder Ahoy

RIP: Departed Businesses and Organizations

People often ask us, "Whatever happened to...?" Here is a list of entries that have been dropped since our last edition. Anyone with additional information is invited to contact the editor.

Booksellers

Abbey Books (Toronto ON) - limited selection of mystery
Acorn Books - limited selection of mystery
Alex liest Agatha - unable to confirm
Bang! Bang! Bookclub - lost in cyberspace
Bloody Dagger Books - unable to confirm
Book Nook by the Sea - changed focus
The Book Shelf (Angel Fire NM) - closed
Bud Schweska - unable to confirm
Bunch of Grapes Bookstore - limited selection of mystery
Chronicles Bookshop - unable to confirm
A Compleat Mystery Bookshop - closed
David Poitras, Bookseller - unable to confirm
Frog Hollow Books - unable to confirm
Grey House Books - unable to confirm
Haven't Got a Clue - limited selection of mystery
Henri Labelle - lost in cyberspace
McNeil Books - out of business
Mysteries, Movies & Mayhem - unable to confirm
Mystery Books (Bryn Mawr PA) - owner retired
MysteryBooks™ (Washington DC) - closed

Associations

The Agatha Christie Society - see AgathaChristie.com under Information Resources
Associazione Italiana Scrittori di Poliziesco - unable to confirm
IACW, Canada - incorrect listing
IACW, Chile - discontinued
IACW, Netherlands - discontinued
The Salon Pistols of Gainesville - unable to confirm
Sovershenno Secretno - unable to confirm

Events

Caledonian Crime - past event
Frenzy Expo - discontinued
Murder on the Maitland - unable to confirm
Mystery: The Florida Connection - past event

Periodicals and Reviewers

Arthur K Amos Jr - unable to confirm
APB News - lost in cyberspace
Blue Murder Magazine - no longer published
Clues: A Journal of Detection - no longer published
Crime.com - discontinued

Carol Harper - unable to confirm
JDM Bibliophile - owner deceased
Kriminallitterære Nyheder - no longer published
Lawrence Block Newsletter - now email only
Max Allan Collins Newsletter - no longer published
Meritorious Mysteries - no recent publications
Mysterious Discoveries - no recent publications
Mystery & Adventure Series Review - no recent publications
Mystery Time - owner retired
Nefarious—Tales of Mystery - no recent publications
Over My Dead Body! - no recent publications
Paperbacks, Pulps & Comics - publication suspended

Publishers
Avid Press - out of business
Black Hill Books (Publishers) - no recent publications
E-Pulp - lost in cyberspace
Fjord Press - closed
Ichabod Books - unable to confirm
Independent Spirit Publishing - no recent publications
Oak Tree Press - no reply to queries
Out of Bounds Books - unable to confirm
Rare Sound Press - no recent publications
Redfield Publishers - no recent publications
Silver River Inc - no recent publications
Write Way Publishing - publication suspended

Information Resources
Archives of Detective Fiction - seeMercantile Library of New York
BookBrowser - assimilated by Barnes & Noble
University of California, San Diego: Mandeville Special Collections Library - unable to
    confirm mystery-related collections
The MacGuffin Guide to Detective Fiction - discontinued
University of Wisconsin: Madison Memorial Library - limited selection of mystery

Entertainment & Gifts
Accessories to Murder - unable to confirm
Baker Street Emporium - unable to confirm
Clipper Air Cruises - unable to confirm
CruiseWorks, Inc. - unable to confirm
Mystery Theatre Productions - lost in cyberspace
Poets of the Tabloid Murder - discontinued
RadioMystery.com - out of business
Rivertown Trading Company - assimilated by Marshall Fields

GLOSSARY OF ACRONYMS

A&E	Arts & Entertainment Network
ABA	American Booksellers Association
ABA(AU)	Australian Booksellers Association
ABA(UK)	Antiquarian Booksellers Association (UK)
ABAA	Antiquarian Booksellers Association of America
ABAC	Antiquarian Booksellers Association of Canada
AKA	also known as
ARC	advance reader's copy
CBA	Canadian Booksellers Association
CBC	Canadian Broadcasting Corporation
CWA	**Crime Writers Association** (UK)
CWAA	**Crime Writers Association of Australia**
CWC	**Crime Writers of Canada**
GLBA	Great Lakes Booksellers Association
h/c	hardcover
ILAB	International League of Antiquarian Booksellers
IMBA	**Independent Mystery Booksellers of America**
IOBA	Independent Online Booksellers Association
MPBA	Mountains and Plains Booksellers Association
MSIBA	Mid-South Independent Booksellers Association
MSS	manuscripts
MWA	**Mystery Writers of America**
NAIBA	New Atlantic Independent Booksellers Association
NCIBA	Northern California Independent Booksellers Association
NEBA	New England Booksellers Association
NHABA	New Hampshire Antiquarian Booksellers Association
NTBA	North Texas Booksellers Association
p/b	paperback
PBS	Public Broadcasting System
PW	Publishers Weekly
RMABA	Rocky Mountain Antiquarian Booksellers Association
SEBA	Southeast Booksellers Association
SF	science fiction or (sometimes) speculative fiction
SINC	**Sisters in Crime**
TBD	to be determined

Index

B

C

N

U

V

W

Afterwords

ACKNOWLEDGEMENTS

Many thanks to Sharon Villines, the founder of Deadly Serious Press and originator of the *Deadly Directory;* and to the members of DAPA-EM, for their knowledge and support.

ABOUT THE EDITOR

Kate Derie is a freelance writer and editor who specializes in the mystery fiction field. She is the creator and director of ClueLass.com, a popular Internet site for mystery fiction fans. She is also the Associate Editor of the *Mystery Readers Journal,* and has a regular column in the Sisters in Crime national newsletter.

COLOPHON

The basic text font for the *Deadly Directory* is Adobe Garamond; listing headers are Lithos Bold; and section headers are Brush Script. Graphic icons are adapted from Macintosh Cairo. The database engine for both the print and online editions of the directory is FileMaker Pro, and page layout was done in Adobe InDesign. Printed in the USA.

Printed in the United States
992200003B